Learning Angular

Second Edition

Addison-Wesley Learning Series

LEARNING
REACT

KIRUPA CHINNATHAMBI

SECOND EDITION
LEARNING
Blender
A Hands-On Guide to Creating 3D Animated Characters

OLIVER VILLAR

LEARNING TO
PROGRAM

STEVEN FOOTE

THE LANGUAGE of SQL
SECOND EDITION

LARRY ROCKOFF

Visit **informit.com/learningseries** for a complete list of available publications.

The **Addison-Wesley Learning Series** is a collection of hands-on programming guides that help you quickly learn a new technology or language so you can apply what you've learned right away.

Each title comes with sample code for the application or applications built in the text. This code is fully annotated and can be reused in your own projects with no strings attached. Many chapters end with a series of exercises to encourage you to reexamine what you have just learned, and to tweak or adjust the code as a way of learning.

Titles in this series take a simple approach: they get you going right away and leave you with the ability to walk off and build your own application and apply the language or technology to whatever you are working on.

Make sure to connect with us!
informit.com/socialconnect

Pearson
Addison-Wesley

informIT.com
the trusted technology learning source

O'REILLY®
Safari

Learning Angular

Second Edition

Brad Dayley
Brendan Dayley
Caleb Dayley

✦ Addison-Wesley

Learning Angular, Second Edition

ISBN-13: 978-0-134-57697-8

ISBN-10: 0-134-57697-7

Library of Congress Control Number: 2017953922

Printed in the United States of America

1 17

Trademarks

Warning and Disclaimer

Special Sales

For information about buying this title in bulk quantities, or for special sales opportunities (which may include electronic versions; custom cover designs; and content particular to your business, training goals, marketing focus, or branding interests), please contact our corporate sales department at corpsales@pearsoned.com or (800) 382-3419.

For government sales inquiries, please contact governmentsales@pearsoned.com.

For questions about sales outside the U.S., please contact intlcs@pearson.com.

Editor
Mark Taber

Managing Editor
Sandra Schroeder

Project Editor
Lori Lyons

Copy Editor
Kitty Wilson

Indexer
Erika Millen

Technical Editor
Jesse Smith

Project Manager
Dhayanidhi Karunanidhi

Cover Designer
Chuti Prasertsith

Contents at a Glance

Contents

About the Authors

Brad Dayley is a senior software engineer with more than 20 years of experience developing enterprise applications and web interfaces. He has used JavaScript and jQuery for years and is the author of *Node.JS, MongoDB, and Angular Web Development*, *jQuery and JavaScript Phrasebook* and *Sams Teach Yourself AngularJS, JavaScript, and jQuery All in One*. He has designed and implemented a wide array of applications and services, from application servers to complex web applications.

Brendan Dayley is a web application developer who loves learning and implementing the latest and greatest technologies. He is the co-author of *Sams Teach Yourself AngularJS, JavaScript, and jQuery All in One* and *Node.JS, MongoDB, and Angular Web Development*. He has written a number of web applications using JavaScript, TypeScript, and Angular, and he is exploring the capabilities of new web and mobile technologies such as augmented reality and how to use them for innovative solutions.

Caleb Dayley is a university student who is studying computer science. Introduced to software development at a young age, he has taught himself much of what he knows about computer programming. He is a developer in JavaScript, Python, and C#, and is a big fan of the Unity platform. He is also the co-author of *Node.JS, MongoDB, and Angular Web Development*. He is excited for what the future holds, and the opportunities to help design and create the next generation of innovative software that will continue to improve the way we live, work, and play.

Acknowledgments

I'd like to take this page to thank all those who made this book possible. First, I thank my wonderful wife for the inspiration, love, and support she give me. I'd never have made it this far without you. I also want to thank my boys for the help they are when I am writing. Thanks to Mark Taber for getting this title rolling in the right direction.

— *Brad Dayley*

We Want to Hear from You!

As the reader of this book, *you* are our most important critic and commentator. We value your opinion and want to know what we're doing right, what we could do better, what areas you'd like to see us publish in, and any other words of wisdom you're willing to pass our way.

You can email or write directly to let us know what you did or didn't like about this book—as well as what we can do to make our books stronger.

Please note that we cannot help you with technical problems related to the topic of this book and that due to the high volume of mail we receive, we might not be able to reply to every message.

When you write, please be sure to include this book's title and author, as well as your name and phone or email address.

Email: feedback@developers-library.info

Mail: Reader Feedback
Addison-Wesley Developer's Library
800 East 96th Street
Indianapolis, IN 46240 USA

Reader Services

Visit our website and register this book at **www.informit.com/register** for convenient access to any updates, downloads, or errata that might be available for this book.

Accessing the Free Web Edition

Your purchase of this book in any format includes access to the corresponding Web Edition, which provides several special online-only features:

- The complete text of the book
- Updates and corrections as they become available

The Web Edition can be viewed on all types of computers and mobile devices with any modern web browser that supports HTML5.

To get access to the *Learning Angular* Web Edition all you need to do is register this book:

1. Go to www.informit.com/register
2. Sign in or create a new account.
3. Enter ISBN: **9780134576978**
4. Answer the questions as proof of purchase.
5. The Web Edition will appear under the Digital Purchases tab on your Account page. Click the Launch link to access the product.

Introduction

Welcome to *Learning Angular*. This book is designed to catapult you into the world of using Angular to build highly interactive and well-structured web applications. The book covers the basics of the Angular framework and how to use it to build well-designed, reusable components for web applications. Angular is one of the most exciting and innovative technologies emerging in the world of web development.

This introduction covers the following:

- Who should read this book
- Why you should read this book
- What you will be able to achieve using this book
- What Angular is and why it is a great technology
- How this book is organized
- Where to find the code examples

Let's get started.

Who Should Read This Book

This book is aimed at readers who already have an understanding of the basics of HTML and have done some programming in a modern programming language. Having a current understanding of JavaScript will make this book easier to digest but is not required as the basics of JavaScript are covered here.

Why You Should Read This Book

This book will teach you how to create powerful, interactive web applications that have a well-structured, easy-to-reuse code base that is easy to maintain. A great feature about Angular is that it actually forces you to become a better web developer by adhering to the underlying structure and design.

The typical readers of this book want to master Angular for the purpose of building highly interactive web applications. Typical readers will also want to leverage the innovative Model View Controller (MVC) approach of Angular to implement well-designed and structured web pages and web applications. Overall, Angular provides an easy-to-implement, fully integrated web development platform that enables you to implement amazing Web 2.0 applications.

What You Will Learn from This Book

This book will teach you how to build real-world, dynamic websites and web applications. Websites are no longer formed of simple static content—HTML pages with integrated images and formatted text. Instead, websites have become much more dynamic, with a single page often serving as an entire site or application.

Using Angular technology enables you to build logic directly into your web page to bind the data model for the client web application to back-end services and databases. Angular also enables you to easily extend the capability of HTML so that the UI design logic can be expressed easily in an HTML template file. Following are just a few of the things you will learn while reading this book:

- How to quickly build Angular templates with built-in directives that enhance the user experience
- How to bind UI elements to the data model so that when the model changes, the UI changes and vice versa
- How to bind mouse and keyboard events directly to the data model and back-end functionality to provide robust user interactions
- How to define your own custom Angular directives that extend the HTML language
- How to implement client-side services that can interact with the web server
- How to build dynamic browser views that provide rich user interaction
- How to create custom services that can easily be reused in other Angular applications
- How to implement rich UI components such as zoomable images and expandable lists as custom Angular directives

What Is Angular?

Angular is a client-side JavaScript framework developed mostly by Google. The entire ideology behind Angular is to provide a framework that makes it easy to implement well-designed and well-structured web pages and applications using an MVC or Model View View Model (MVVM) framework.

Angular provides all that functionality to handle user input in the browser, manipulate data on the client side, and control how elements are displayed in the browser view. Here are some of the benefits Angular provides:

- **Data binding:** Angular has a very clean method for binding data to HTML elements, using its powerful scope mechanism.
- **Extensibility:** The Angular architecture enables you to easily extend almost every aspect of the language to provide your own custom implementations.

- **Clean code:** Angular forces you to write clean, logical code.

- **Reusable code:** The combination of extensibility and clean code makes it very easy to write reusable code in Angular. In fact, the language often forces you to do so when you're creating custom services.

- **Support:** Google is investing a lot into this project, which gives it an advantage where other similar initiatives have failed.

- **Compatibility:** Angular is based on JavaScript and has a close relationship with the JavaScript standard. That makes it easier to begin integrating Angular into your environment and reuse pieces of your existing code within the structure of the Angular framework.

How This Book Is Organized

This book is divided into 12 chapters.

Chapter 1, "Jumping into JavaScript," provides a JavaScript primer, just in case you are not familiar with JavaScript. This chapter also walks you through the process of setting up a development environment. You should at least check out the first few sections, even if you are familiar with JavaScript, so that you can create the development environment.

Chapter 2, "Jumping into TypeScript," provides an additional primer on TypeScript, which is a superset of JavaScript. The majority of Angular examples, including the ones in this book, are written in TypeScript, so it is a must for developing with Angular.

Chapter 3, "Getting Started with Angular," covers the basics of the Angular framework. You will learn how Angular is organized and how to design Angular applications.

Chapter 4, "Angular Components," covers the basic structure of Angular components, which are the building blocks of Angular. You will learn how to create components using HTML templates and JavaScript.

Chapter 5, "Expressions," covers using expressions and pipes in Angular templates. You will learn about the built-in expression syntax and pipes as well as how to create your own.

Chapter 6, "Data Binding," covers the basics of binding data in an Angular component to UI elements in an HTML template.

Chapter 7, "Built-in Directives," covers the directives that are built into Angular. Directives allow you to change the structure of DOM elements as well as utilize HTTP attributes.

Chapter 8, "Custom Directives," covers building your own custom directives to extend HTML. You will learn about attribute directives and how to use directives with components.

Chapter 9, "Events and Change Detection," covers the types of events you will encounter in Angular and how to manage them. You will learn how to create and handle your own custom events. This chapter also covers how to use observables to watch for and react to data changes in your web applications.

Chapter 10, "Implementing Angular Services in Web Applications," covers the built-in services that Angular provides. These services enable you to communicate with the web server using HTTP requests, implement routing to navigate application view changes, and implement animations on web pages.

Chapter 11, "Creating Your Own Custom Angular Services," covers the mechanics available in Angular to create your own custom services. Custom services enable you to make functionality reusable because you can easily inject the functionality provided by these services into multiple applications.

Chapter 12, "Having Fun with Angular," provides several examples of using Angular to create rich UI components in real-world examples. You will get a chance to see how to implement drag and drop, animations, and other UI elements.

Getting the Code Examples

Throughout this book, you will find code examples contained in listings. The title of each listing includes the filename of the file that contains the listing's source code. You can access the source code files and images used in the examples at the book's website (see the back cover).

Finally

Enjoy this book and enjoy learning about Angular. It is a great, innovative technology that is really fun to use. Soon you'll be able to join the many other web developers who use Angular to build interactive websites and web applications.

Jumping into JavaScript

Angular is built on TypeScript, which is a superset of JavaScript. It is important for you to have a basic understanding of JavaScript before you can jump into the Angular world. This chapter has two purposes: to show you how to set up a development environment and to teach you the basics of JavaScript.

The first part of this chapter discusses the necessary basics of setting up a JavaScript development environment. You should at least take a quick look at this section even if you already are familiar with JavaScript and have a development environment set up.

The rest of this chapter familiarizes you with some of the language basics of JavaScript, such as variables, functions, and objects. It is not intended as a full language guide but rather a synopsis of important syntax and idioms. If you are not familiar with JavaScript, working through this primer should enable you to understand the examples throughout the rest of the book. If you already know JavaScript well, you can either skip those sections or review them as a refresher.

Setting Up a JavaScript Development Environment

There are so many ways to set up a JavaScript development environment that it is difficult to focus on just one. Most good integrated development environment (IDE) tools provide at least some sort of capability to easily set up a JavaScript development environment. So if you have a favorite IDE, you should check out its JavaScript capabilities.

To effectively build Angular applications using JavaScript and/or TypeScript, your development environment needs to have the following components:

- **Editor:** The editor enables you to create the necessary JavaScript, HTML, and CSS files to build an Angular application. There are a lot of editors out there, and you can pick one you are familiar with. This book uses Visual Studio Code because it has built-in compatibility for TypeScript.

- **Browser:** You need a web browser to test and try your applications. For the most part, JavaScript and Angular applications run in the same way across the major browsers.

Angular supports ECMAScript 5 and 6, and most modern browsers have the majority of ECMAScript 6 implemented. However, there is some functionality which does not work the same in older browsers. It is always a good idea to test your applications in the major browsers that your customers will use to ensure that it works correctly in all of them.

Defining Variables

You use variables in JavaScript to temporarily store and access data from your JavaScript files. Variables can point to simple data types such as numbers or strings, or they can point to more complex data types such as objects.

To define a variable in JavaScript, you use the `var` keyword and then give the variable a name, as in this example:

```
var myData;
```

You can also assign a value to the variable in the same line. For example, the following line of code creates a variable `myString` and assigns the value `"Some Text"` to it:

```
var myString = "Some Text";
```

The following two lines do the same thing:

```
var myString;
myString = "Some Text";
```

After you have declared a variable, you can use its name to assign a value to the variable and access the value of the variable. For example, the following code stores a string in the `myString` variable and then uses it when assigning the value to the `newString` variable:

```
var myString = "Some Text";
var newString = myString + " Some More Text";
```

You should give variables descriptive names so that you know later what data they store and can more easily use them in your programs. A variable name must begin with a letter, $, or _, and it cannot contain spaces. In addition, variable names are case sensitive, so, for example, `myString` is different from `MyString`.

Understanding JavaScript Data Types

JavaScript uses data types to determine how to handle data that is assigned to a variable. The variable type determines what operations you can perform on the variable, such as looping or executing. The following list describes the types of variables that you will most commonly work with in this book:

- **String:** This data type stores character data as a string. The character data is specified with either single or double quotation marks. All the data contained in the quotes is assigned to the string variable. Consider these examples:
  ```
  var myString = 'Some Text';
  var anotherString = 'Some More Text';
  ```

- **Number:** This data type stores data as a numeric value. Numbers are useful in counting, calculations, and comparisons. The following are examples:

```
var myInteger = 1;
var cost = 1.33;
```

- **Boolean:** This data type stores a single bit that is either `true` or `false`. Booleans are often used for flags. For example, you might set a variable to `false` at the beginning of some code and then check it on completion to see if the code execution hit a certain spot. The following examples define `true` and `false` variables:

```
var yes = true;
var no = false;
```

- **Array:** An indexed array is a series of separate distinct data items, all stored under a single variable name. JavaScript arrays are heterogeneous, which means they support different types of objects in the same array. Items in the array can be accessed by their zero-based index, using `array[index]`. The following is an example of creating a simple array and then accessing the first element, which is at index `0`:

```
var arr = ["one", "two", "three"];
var first = arr[0];
```

- **Object literal:** JavaScript supports the ability to create and use object literals. When you use an object literal, you can access values and functions in the object by using `object.property` syntax. The following example shows how to create and access properties of an object literal:

```
var obj = {"name": "Brad", "occupation": "Hacker", "age": "Unknown"};
var name = obj.name;
```

- **Null:** Sometimes you do not have a value to store in a variable either because it hasn't been created or you are no longer using it. At such a time, you can set a variable to `null`. Using `null` is better than assigning a value of `0` or an empty string (`""`) because those may be valid values for the variable. In addition, `null` is better than `undefined` because it specifies that a value has been set. By assigning `null` to a variable, you can assign no value and check against `null` inside your code, like this:

```
var newVar = null;
```

Note

JavaScript is not a strongly typed language. That means you do not need to specify in the script the data type of a variable. The interpreter automatically figures out the correct data type for a variable. In addition, you can assign a variable of one type to a value of a different type. For example, the following code defines a string variable and then assigns it to an integer value type:

```
var id = "testID";
id = 1;
```

Using Operators

JavaScript operators allow you to alter the value of a variable. You are already familiar with the = operator used to assign values to variables. JavaScript provides several different operators that fall into two categories: arithmetic and assignment operators.

Arithmetic Operators

You use arithmetic operators to perform operations between variable and direct values. Table 1.1 lists the arithmetic operations, along with the results that are applied.

Table 1.1   JavaScript's Arithmetic Operators, with Results Based on y=4 Initially

Operator	Description	Examples	Resulting x
+	Addition	x=y+5	9
		x=y+"5"	"45"
		x="Four"+y+"4"	"Four44"
-	Subtraction	x=y-2	2
++	Increment	x=y++	4
		x=++y	5
--	Decrement	x=y--	4
		x=--y	3
*	Multiplication	x=y*4	16
/	Division	x=10/y	2.5
%	Modulo (remainder of division)	x=y%3	1

> **Note**
>
> You can also use the + operator to add strings together or to add strings and numbers together. It allows you to quickly concatenate strings as well as add numeric data to output strings. Table 1.1 shows that when you add a numeric value and a string value, the numeric value is converted to a string and then the two strings are concatenated.

Assignment Operators

You use an assignment operator to assign a value to a variable. In addition to the = operator, there are several different forms that allow you to manipulate the data as you assign a value. Table 1.2 lists the assignment operations, along with the results that are applied.

Table 1.2   JavaScript's Assignment Operators, with Results Based on x=10 Initially

Operator	Example	Equivalent Arithmetic Operators	Resulting x
=	x=5	x=5	5
+=	x+=5	x=x+5	15
-=	x-=5	x=x-5	5
*=	x*=5	x=x*5	50
/=	x/=5	x=x/5	2
%=	x%=5	x=x%5	0

Applying Comparison and Conditional Operators

Using conditionals is a way to apply logic to your applications such that certain code will be executed only under specific conditions. You do this by applying comparison logic to variable values. The following sections describe the comparisons available in JavaScript and how to apply them in conditional statements.

Comparison Operators

A comparison operator evaluates two pieces of data and returns true if the evaluation is correct and false if the evaluation is not correct. A comparison operator compares the value on the left of the operator against the value on the right.

Table 1.3 lists the comparison operators and provides some examples.

Table 1.3   JavaScript's Comparison Operators, with Results Based on x=10 Initially

Operator	Description	Examples	Result
==	Equal to (value only)	x==8	false
		x==10	true
===	Both value and type are equal	x===10	true
		x==="10"	false
!=	Not equal	x!=5	true
!==	Both value and type are not equal	x!=="10"	true
		x!==10	false
>	Greater than	x>5	true
>=	Greater than or equal to	x>=10	true
<	Less than	x<5	false
<=	Less than or equal to	x<=10	true

You can chain together multiple comparisons by using logical operators and standard parentheses. Table 1.4 lists the logical operators and shows how to use them to chain together comparisons.

Table 1.4   JavaScript's Comparison Operators, with Results Based on x=10 and y=5 Initially

Operator	Description	Examples	Result
&&	And	(x==10 && y==5)	true
		(x==10 && y>x)	false
||	Or	(x>=10 || y>x)	true
		(x<10 && y>x)	false
!	Not	!(x==y)	true
		!(x>y)	false
	Mix	(x>=10 && y<x || x==y)	true
		((x<y || x>=10) && y>=5)	true
		(!(x==y) && y>=10)	false

Using `if` Statements

An `if` statement allows you to separate code execution based on the evaluation of a comparison. The following lines of code show the conditional operators in () and the code to execute if the conditional evaluates to `true` in {}:

```
if(x==5){
  do_something();
}
```

In addition to only executing code within the `if` statement block, you can specify an `else` block that will be executed only if the condition is `false`. Here is an example:

```
if(x==5){
  do_something();
} else {
  do_something_else();
}
```

You can also chain together `if` statements. To do this, add a conditional statement along with an `else` statement, as in this example:

```
if(x<5){
  do_something();
} else if(x<10) {
  do_something_else();
} else {
  do_nothing();
}
```

Implementing `switch` Statements

Another type of conditional logic is the `switch` statement. The `switch` statement allows you to evaluate an expression once and then, based on the value, execute one of many different sections of code.

The `switch` statement has the following syntax:

```
switch(expression){
  case value1:
    <code to execute>
    break;
  case value2:
    <code to execute>
    break;
  default:
    <code to execute if not value1 or value2>
}
```

Here is what happens: The `switch` statement evaluates the expression entirely and gets a value. The value may be a string, a number, a Boolean, or even an object. The `switch` expression is then compared to each value specified by the `case` statement. If a value matches, the code in the `case` statement is executed. If no values match, the default code is executed.

> **Note**
>
> Typically each `case` statement includes a `break` command at the end to signal a break out of the `switch` statement. If no `break` is found, code execution continues with the next `case` statement.

Implementing Looping

Looping is a means to execute the same segment of code multiple times. It is extremely useful when you need to repeatedly perform the same tasks on an array or a set of objects.

JavaScript provides functionality to perform `for` and `while` loops, as described in the following sections.

`while` Loops

The most basic type of looping in JavaScript is accomplished with the `while` loop. A `while` loop tests an expression and continues to execute the code contained in its {} brackets until the expression evaluates to `false`.

For example, the following `while` loop executes until i is equal to 5:

```
var i = 1;
while (i<5){
  console.log("Iteration " + i);
  i++;
}
```

This example sends the following output to the console:

```
Iteration 1
Iteration 2
Iteration 3
Iteration 4
```

do/while **Loops**

Another type of `while` loop is the do/while loop, which is useful if you always want to execute the code in the loop at least once and the expression cannot be tested until the code has executed at least once.

For example, the following do/while loop executes until days is equal to Wednesday:

```
var days = ["Monday", "Tuesday", "Wednesday", "Thursday", "Friday"];
var i=0;
do{
  var day=days[i++];
  console.log("It's " + day);
} while (day != "Wednesday");
```

This is the output at the console:

```
It's Monday
It's Tuesday
It's Wednesday
```

for **Loops**

A JavaScript `for` loop allows you to execute code a specific number of times by using a `for` statement that combines three statements in a single block of execution. Here's the syntax:

```
for (assignment; condition; update;){
  code to be executed;
}
```

The `for` statement uses the three statements as follows when executing the loop:

- *assignment*: This is executed before the loop begins and not again. It is used to initialize variables that will be used in the loop as conditionals.

- *condition*: This expression is evaluated before each iteration of the loop. If the expression evaluates to true, the loop is executed; otherwise, the `for` loop execution ends.

- *update:* This is executed on each iteration, after the code in the loop has executed. This is typically used to increment a counter that is used in `condition`.

The following example illustrates a `for` loop and the nesting of one loop inside another:

```
for (var x=1; x<=3; x++){
  for (var y=1; y<=3; y++){
    console.log(x + " X " + y + " = " + (x*y));
  }
}
```

This example sends the following output to the web console:

```
1 X 1 = 1
1 X 2 = 2
1 X 3 = 3
2 X 1 = 2
2 X 2 = 4
2 X 3 = 6
3 X 1 = 3
3 X 2 = 6
3 X 3 = 9
```

`for/in` Loops

Another type of `for` loop is the `for/in` loop. The `for/in` loop executes on any data type that can be iterated. For the most part, you use `for/in` loops on arrays and objects. The following example illustrates the syntax and behavior of the `for/in` loop on a simple array:

```
var days = ["Monday", "Tuesday", "Wednesday", "Thursday", "Friday"];
for (var idx in days){
  console.log("It's " + days[idx] + "<br>");
}
```

Notice that the variable `idx` is adjusted each iteration through the loop, from the beginning array index to the last. This is the resulting output:

```
It's Monday
It's Tuesday
It's Wednesday
It's Thursday
It's Friday
```

Interrupting Loops

When you work with loops, there are times when you need to interrupt the execution of code inside the code itself, without waiting for the next iteration. There are two different ways to do this: by using the `break` keyword and by using the `continue` keyword.

The break keyword completely stops execution of a `for` or `while` loop. The `continue` keyword, on the other hand, stops execution of the code inside the loop and continues on with the next iteration. Consider the following examples.

This example shows using `break` if the day is Wednesday:

```
var days = ["Monday", "Tuesday", "Wednesday", "Thursday", "Friday"];
for (var idx in days){
  if (days[idx] == "Wednesday")
    break;
  console.log("It's " + days[idx] + "<br>");
}
```

Once the value is `Wednesday`, loop execution stops completely:

```
It's Monday
It's Tuesday
```

This example shows using `continue` if the day is Wednesday:

```
var days = ["Monday", "Tuesday", "Wednesday", "Thursday", "Friday"];
for (var idx in days){
  if (days[idx] == "Wednesday")
    continue;
  console.log("It's " + days[idx] + "<br>");
}
```

Notice that the write is not executed for `Wednesday` because of the `continue` statement, but the loop execution completes:

```
It's Monday
It's Tuesday
It's Thursday
It's Friday
```

Creating Functions

One of the most important parts of JavaScript is making code that other code can reuse. To do this, you organize your code into functions that perform specific tasks. A function is a series of code statements combined together in a single block and given a name. You can execute the code in the block by referencing that name.

Defining Functions

You define a function by using the `function` keyword followed by a name that describes the use of the function, a list of zero or more arguments in `()`, and a block of one or more code statements in `{}`. For example, the following is a function definition that writes `"Hello World"` to the console:

```
function myFunction(){
  console.log("Hello World");
}
```

To execute the code in `myFunction()`, all you need to do is add the following line to the main JavaScript or inside another function:

```
myFunction();
```

Passing Variables to Functions

Frequently you need to pass specific values to functions, and the functions use those values when executing their code. You pass values to a function in comma-delimited form. A function definition needs a list of variable names in `()` that match the number of arguments being passed in. For example, the following function accepts two arguments, *name* and *city*, and uses them to build the output string:

```
function greeting(name, city){
  console.log("Hello " + name);
  console.log(". How is the weather in " + city);
}
```

To call the `greeting()` function, you need to pass in a *name* value and a *city* value. The value can be a direct value or a previously defined variable. To illustrate this, the following code executes the `greeting()` function with a *name* variable and a direct string for *city*:

```
var name = "Brad";
greeting(name, "Florence");
```

Returning Values from Functions

Often, a function needs to return a value to the calling code. Adding a `return` keyword followed by a variable or value returns that value from the function. For example, the following code calls a function to format a string, assigns the value returned from the function to a variable, and then writes the value to the console:

```
function formatGreeting(name, city){
  var retStr = "";
  retStr += "Hello <b>" + name + "/n");
  retStr += "Welcome to " + city + "!";
return retStr;
}
var greeting = formatGreeting("Brad", "Rome");
console.log(greeting);
```

You can include more than one `return` statement in the function. When the function encounters a `return` statement, code execution of the function stops immediately. If the `return` statement contains a value to return, then that value is returned. The following example shows a function that tests the input and returns immediately if it is zero:

```
function myFunc(value){
  if (value == 0)
    return value;
  <code_to_execute_if_value_nonzero>
  return value;
}
```

Using Anonymous Functions

So far, all the examples in this chapter have shown named functions. JavaScript also lets you create anonymous functions. These functions have the advantage of being defined directly in the parameter sets when you call other functions, and thus you do not need formal definitions.

For example, the following code defines a function `doCalc()` that accepts three parameters. The first two should be numbers, and the third is a function that will be called and passed the two numbers as arguments:

```
function doCalc(num1, num2, calcFunction){
    return calcFunction(num1, num2);
}
```

You could define a function and then pass the function name without parameters to `doCalc()`, as in this example:

```
function addFunc(n1, n2){
    return n1 + n2;
}
doCalc(5, 10, addFunc);
```

However, you also have the option of using an anonymous function directly in the call to `doCalc()`, as shown in these two statements:

```
console.log( doCalc(5, 10, function(n1, n2){ return n1 + n2; }) );
console.log( doCalc(5, 10, function(n1, n2){ return n1 * n2; }) );
```

You can probably see that the advantage of using anonymous functions is that you do not need a formal definition that will not be used anywhere else in your code. Anonymous functions, therefore, make JavaScript code more concise and readable. A function passed in as a parameter and called from inside is known as a *callback function*. A big advantage of using a callback function is that the initial function does not need to know anything about the function that will be executed, so you have more flexibility.

Understanding Variable Scope

Once you start adding conditions, functions, and loops to your JavaScript applications, you need to understand variable scoping. Variable scoping sets out to determine the value of a specific variable name at the line of code currently being executed.

JavaScript allows you to define both a global version and a local version of a variable. The global version is defined in the main JavaScript, and local versions are defined inside functions. When you define a local version in a function, a new variable is created in memory. Within that function, you reference the local version. Outside that function, you reference the global version.

To understand variable scoping a bit better, consider the code in Listing 1.1.

Listing 1.1   **Defining Global and Local Variables in JavaScript**

```
01 var myVar = 1;
02 function writeIt(){
03   var myVar = 2;
04   console.log("Variable = " + myVar);
05   writeMore();
06 }
07 function writeMore(){
08   console.log("Variable = " + myVar);
09 }
10 writeIt();
```

The global variable `myVar` is defined on line 1, and a local version is defined on line 3, within the `writeIt()` function. Line 4 writes `"Variable = 2"` to the console. Then in line 5, `writeMore()` is called. Because there is no local version of `myVar` defined in `writeMore()`, the value of the global `myVar` is written in line 9.

Using JavaScript Objects

JavaScript has several built-in objects, such as `Number`, `Array`, `String`, `Date`, and `Math`. Each of these built-in objects has member properties and methods. In addition to the JavaScript objects, you will find as you read this book that TypeScript and Angular add their own built-in objects as well.

JavaScript provides a fairly nice object-oriented programming structure for you to create your own custom objects as well. Using objects rather than just a collection of functions is key to writing clean, efficient, reusable JavaScript code.

Using Object Syntax

To use objects in JavaScript effectively, you need to have an understanding of their structure and syntax. An object is really just a container to group together multiple values and, in some instances, functions. The values of objects are called *properties*, and the values of functions are called *methods*.

To use a JavaScript object, you must first create an instance of the object. You create object instances by using the `new` keyword with the object constructor name. For example, to create a `Number` object, you could use the following line of code:

```
var x = new Number("5");
```

Object syntax is very straightforward: You use the object name and then a dot and then the property or method name. For example, the following lines of code get and set the `name` property of an object named `myObj`:

```
var s = myObj.name;
myObj.name = "New Name";
```

You can also get and set object methods of an object in the same manner. For example, the following lines of code call the `getName()` method and then change the method function on an object named `myObj`:

```
var name = myObj.getName();
myObj.getName = function() { return this.name; };
```

You can also create objects and assign variables and functions directly by using {} syntax. For example, the following code defines a new object and assigns values and a method function:

```
var obj = {
    name: "My Object",
    value: 7,
    getValue: function() { return this.name; };
};
```

You can also access members of a JavaScript object by using the *object* [*propertyName*] syntax. This is useful when you are using dynamic property names and when a property name must include characters that JavaScript does not support. For example, the following examples access the `"User Name"` and `"Other Name"` properties of an object name `myObj`:

```
var propName = "User Name";
var val1 = myObj[propName];
var val2 = myObj["Other Name"];
```

Creating Custom Defined Objects

As you have seen so far, using the built-in JavaScript objects has several advantages. As you begin to write code that uses more and more data, you will find yourself wanting to build your own custom objects, with specific properties and methods.

You can define JavaScript objects in a couple different ways. The simplest is the on-the-fly method: Simply create a generic object and then add properties to it as needed. For example, to create a user object and assign a first and last name as well as define a function to return them, you could use the following code:

```
var user = new Object();
user.first="Brad";
user.last="Dayley";
user.getName = function( ) { return this.first + " " + this.last; }
```

You could also accomplish the same effect through direct assignment, using the following code, where the object is enclosed in {} and the properties are defined using *property*:*value* syntax. This method is referred to as object literal notation:

```
var user = {
  first: 'Brad',
  last: 'Dayley',
  getName: function( ) { return this.first + " " + this.last; }};
```

These first two options work very well for simple objects that you do not need to reuse later. A better method for reusable objects is to actually enclose an object inside its own function block.

This has the advantage of allowing you to keep all the code pertaining to the object local to the object itself. Here is an example:

```
function User(first, last){
  this.first = first;
  this.last = last;
  this.getName = function( ) { return this.first + " " + this.last; };
var user = new User("Brad", "Dayley");
```

The end result of these methods is essentially the same as if you have an object with properties that can be referenced using dot notation, as shown here:

```
console.log(user.getName());
```

Using a Prototyping Object Pattern

An even more advanced method of creating objects is by using a prototyping pattern. You implement such a pattern by defining the functions inside the prototype attribute of the object instead of inside the object itself. With prototyping, the functions defined in the prototype are created only once, when the JavaScript is loaded, instead of each time a new object is created.

The following example shows the prototyping syntax:

```
function UserP(first, last){
  this.first = first;
  this.last = last;
}
UserP.prototype = {
  getFullName: function(){
      return this.first + " " + this.last;
  }
};
```

Notice that you define the object UserP and then set UserP.prototype to include the getFullName() function. You can include as many functions in the prototype as you like. Each time a new object is created, those functions are available.

Manipulating Strings

The String object is by far the most commonly used object in JavaScript. JavaScript automatically creates a String object for you any time you define a variable that has a string data type, as in this example:

```
var myStr = "Teach Yourself jQuery & JavaScript in 24 Hours";
```

When you create a string, there are a few special characters that you can't add directly to the string. For those characters, JavaScript provides a set of escape codes, listed in Table 1.5.

Table 1.5 **String Object Escape Codes**

Escape Code	Description	Example	Output String
\'	Single quotation mark	"couldn\'t be"	couldn't be
\"	Double quotation mark	"I \"think\" I \"am\""	I "think" I "am"
\\	Backslash	"one\\two\\three"	one\two\three
\n	New line	"I am\nI said"	I am I said
\r	Carriage return	"to be\ror not"	to be or not
\t	Tab	"one\ttwo\tthree"	one two three
\b	Backspace	"correctoin\b\b\bion"	correction
\f	Form feed	"Title A\fTitle B"	Title A then Title B

To determine the length of a string, you can use the length property of the String object, as in this example:

```
var numOfChars = myStr.length;
```

The String object has several functions that allow you to access and manipulate a string in various ways. The methods for string manipulation are described in Table 1.6.

Table 1.6 **Methods to Manipulate String Objects**

Method	Description
charAt(index)	Returns the character at the specified index.
charCodeAt(index)	Returns the Unicode value of the character at the specified index.
concat(str1, str2, ...)	Joins two or more strings and returns a copy of the joined strings.
fromCharCode()	Converts Unicode values to actual characters.
indexOf(subString)	Returns the position of the first occurrence of a specified subString value. Returns -1 if the substring is not found.
lastIndexOf(subString)	Returns the position of the last occurrence of a specified subString value. Returns -1 if the substring is not found.
match(regex)	Searches the string and returns all matches to the regular expression.
replace(subString/regex, replacementString)	Searches the string for a match of the substring or regular expression and replaces the matched substring with a new substring.

Method	Description
`search(regex)`	Searches the string, based on the regular expression, and returns the position of the first match.
`slice(start, end)`	Returns a new string that has the portion of the string between the `start` and `end` positions removed.
`split(sep, limit)`	Splits a string into an array of substrings, based on a separator character or regular expression. The optional `limit` argument defines the maximum number of splits to make, starting from the beginning.
`substr(start,length)`	Extracts the characters from a string, beginning at a specified `start` position and through the specified `length` of characters.
`substring(from, to)`	Returns a substring of characters between the `from` and `to` index values.
`toLowerCase()`	Converts the string to lowercase.
`toUpperCase()`	Converts the string to uppercase.
`valueOf()`	Returns the primitive string value.

To get you started on using the functionality provided in the `String` object, the following sections describe some of the common tasks that can be done using `String` object methods.

Combining Strings

You can combine multiple strings either by using a + operation or by using the `concat()` function on the first string. For example, in the following code, `sentence1` and `sentence2` will be the same:

```
var word1 = "Today ";
var word2 = "is ";
var word3 = "tomorrows\' ";
var word4 = "yesterday.";
var sentence1 = word1 + word2 + word3 + word4;
var sentence2 = word1.concat(word2, word3, word4);
```

Searching a String for a Substring

To determine whether a string is a substring of another, you can use the `indexOf()` method. For example, the following code writes the string to the console only if it contains the word think:

```
var myStr = "I think, therefore I am.";
if (myStr.indexOf("think") != -1){
  console.log (myStr);
}
```

Replacing a Word in a String

Another common `string` object task is replacing one substring with another. To replace a word or phrase in a string, you use the `replace()` method. The following code replaces the text `"<username>"` with the value of the variable `username`:

```
var username = "Brad";
var output = "<username> please enter your password: ";
output.replace("<username>", username);
```

Splitting a String into an Array

A very common task with strings is to split them into arrays, using a separator character. For example, the following code splits a time string into an array of its basic parts, using the `split()` method on the `":"` separator:

```
var t = "12:10:36";
var tArr = t.split(":");
var hour = tArr[0];
var minute = tArr[1];
var second = tArr[2];
```

Working with Arrays

The `Array` object provides a means of storing and handling a set of other objects. Arrays can store numbers, strings, or other JavaScript objects. There are a couple different ways to create JavaScript arrays. For example, the following statements create three identical versions of the same array:

```
var arr = ["one", "two", "three"];
var arr2 = new Array();
arr2[0] = "one";
arr2[1] = "two";
arr3[2] = "three";
var arr3 = new Array();
arr3.push("one");
arr3.push("two");
arr3.push("three");
```

The first method defines `arr` and sets the contents in a single statement, using `[]`. The second method creates the `arr2` object and then adds items to it, using direct index assignment. The third method creates the `arr3` object and then uses the best option for extending arrays: It uses the `push()` method to push items onto the array.

To determine the number of elements in an array, you can use the `length` property of the `Array` object, as in this example:

```
var numOfItems = arr.length;
```

Arrays follow a zero-based index, meaning that the first item is at index 0 and so on. For example, in the following code, the value of variable first will be Monday, and the value of variable last will be Friday:

```
var
week = ["Monday", "Tuesday", "Wednesday", "Thursday", "Friday"];
var first = w [0];
var last = week[week.length-1];
```

The Array object has several built-in functions that allow you to access and manipulate arrays in various ways. Table 1.7 describes the methods attached to the Array object that allow you to manipulate array contents.

Table 1.7   **Methods to Manipulate Array Objects**

Method	Description
concat(arr1, arr2, ...)	Returns a joined copy of the array and the arrays passed as arguments.
indexOf(value)	Returns the first index of the value in the array or -1 if the item is not found.
join(separator)	Joins all elements of an array, separated by the separator into a single string. If no separator is specified, a comma is used.
lastIndexOf(value)	Returns the last index of the value in the array or -1 if the value is not found.
pop()	Removes the last element from the array and returns that element.
push(item1, item2, ...)	Adds one or more new elements to the end of an array and returns the new length.
reverse()	Reverses the order of all elements in the array.
shift()	Removes the first element of an array and returns that element.
slice(start, end)	Returns the elements between the start and end indexes.
sort(sortFunction)	Sorts the elements of the array. sortFunction is optional.
splice(index, count, item1, item2...)	At the index specified, removes count number of items and then inserts at index any optional items passed in as arguments.
toString()	Returns the string form of an array.
unshift()	Adds new elements to the beginning of an array and returns the new length.
valueOf()	Returns the primitive value of an Array object.

To get you started using the functionality provided in the `Array` object, the following sections describe some of the common tasks that can be done using `Array` object methods.

Combining Arrays

You can combine arrays into a single array by using the `concat()` method but not the `+` method. In the following code, the variable `arr3` contains a string representation of the elements in `arr1` added to a string representation of the elements in `arr2`. The variable `arr4` in the following code is an array with the combined elements from `arr1` and `arr2`:

```
var arr1 = [1,2,3];
var arr2 = ["three", "four", "five"]
var arr3 = arr1 + arr2;
var arr4 = arr1.concat(arr2);
```

> **Note**
>
> You can combine an array of numbers and an array of strings. Each item in the array will keep its own object type. However, as you use the items in the array, you need to keep track of arrays that have more than one data type so that you do not run into problems.

Iterating Through Arrays

You can iterate through an array by using a `for` or a `for/in` loop. The following code illustrates iterating through each item in the array using each method:

```
var week = ["Monday", "Tuesday", "Wednesday", "Thursday", "Friday"];
for (var i=0; i<week.length; i++){
  console.log("<li>" + week[i] + "</li>");
}
for (dayIndex in week){
  console.log("<li>" + week[dayIndex] + "</li>");
}
```

Converting an Array into a String

A very useful feature of `Array` objects is the ability to combine the elements of a string together to make a `String` object, separated by a specific separator using the `join()` method. For example, the following code joins the time components back together into the format `12:10:36`:

```
var timeArr = [12,10,36];
var timeStr = timeArr.join(":");
```

Checking Whether an Array Contains an Item

You often need to check whether an array contains a certain item. You can do this by using the indexOf() method. If the code does not find the item in the list, it returns a -1. The following function writes a message to the console if an item is in the week array:

```
function message(day){
  var week = ["Monday", "Tuesday", "Wednesday", "Thursday", "Friday"];
  if (week.indexOf(day) != -1){
    console.log("Happy " + day);
  }
}
```

Adding Items to and Removing Items from Arrays

There are several methods for adding items to and removing items from Array objects, using the various built-in methods. Table 1.8 shows some of the methods used in this book. The methods are listed in this table as a progression from the beginning of the table to the end.

Table 1.8 **Array Object Methods Used to Add and Remove Elements from Arrays**

Statement	Value of x	Value of arr
var arr = [1,2,3,4,5];	undefined	1,2,3,4,5
var x = 0;	0	1,2,3,4,5
x = arr.unshift("zero");	6 (length)	zero,1,2,3,4,5
x = arr.push(6,7,8);	9 (length)	zero,1,2,3,4,5,6,7,8
x = arr.shift();	zero	1,2,3,4,5,6,7,8
x = arr.pop();	8	1,2,3,4,5,6,7
x = arr.splice(3,3,"four", "five","six");	4,5,6	1,2,3,four,five,six,7
x = arr.splice(3,1);	four	1,2,3,five,six,7
x = arr.splice(3);	five,six,7	1,2,3

Adding Error Handling

An important part of JavaScript coding is adding error handling for instances where there may be problems. By default, if a code exception occurs because of a problem in your JavaScript, the script fails and does not finish loading. This is not usually the desired behavior. In fact, it is often catastrophic behavior. To prevent these types of big problems, you should wrap your code in a try/catch block.

try/catch **Blocks**

To prevent your code from totally bombing out, use `try/catch` blocks that can handle problems inside the code. If JavaScript encounters an error when executing code in a `try` block, it will jump down and execute the `catch` portion instead of stopping the entire script. If no error occurs, the whole `try` block will be executed, and none of the `catch` block will be executed.

For example, the following `try/catch` block tries to assign variable x to a value of an undefined variable named `badVarNam`:

```
try{
    var x = badVarName;
} catch (err){
    console.log(err.name + ': "' + err.message +  '" occurred when assigning x.');
}
```

Notice that the `catch` statement accepts an `err` parameter, which is an error object. The error object provides the `message` property, which provides a description of the error. The error object also provides a `name` property that is the name of the error type that was thrown.

The code above results in an exception and the following message:

```
ReferenceError: "badVarName is not defined" occurred when assigning x.
```

Throwing Your Own Errors

You can throw your own errors by using a `throw` statement. The following code illustrates how to add `throw` statements to a function to throw an error, even if a script error does not occur. The function `sqrRoot()` accepts a single argument x. It then tests x to verify that it is a `positive` number and returns a string with the square root of x. If x is not a positive number, then the appropriate error is thrown, and the `catch` block returns the error:

```
function sqrRoot(x) {
    try {
        if(x=="")     throw {message:"Can't Square Root Nothing"};
        if(isNaN(x)) throw {message:"Can't Square Root Strings"};
        if(x<0)       throw {message:"Sorry No Imagination"};
        return "sqrt("+x+") = " + Math.sqrt(x);
    } catch(err){
        return err.message;
    }
}
function writeIt(){
    console.log(sqrRoot("four"));
    console.log(sqrRoot(""));
    console.log(sqrRoot("4"));
    console.log(sqrRoot("-4"));
}
writeIt();
```

The following is the console output, showing the different errors that are thrown, based on input to the `sqrRoot()` function:

```
Can't Square Root Strings
Can't Square Root Nothing
sqrt(4) = 2
Sorry No Imagination
```

Using `finally`

Another valuable tool in exception handling is the `finally` keyword. You can add this keyword to the end of a `try/catch` block. After the `try/catch` block is executed, the `finally` block is always executed, whether an error occurs and is caught or the `try` block is fully executed. This is especially useful in code that must run no matter what happens in the `try` or `catch` blocks.

Here's an example of using a `finally` block inside a web page:

```
function testTryCatch(value){
  try {
    if (value < 0){
      throw "too small";
    } else if (value > 10){
      throw "too big";
    }
    your_code_here
  } catch (err) {
    console.log("The number was " + err);
  } finally {
    console.log("This is always written.");
  }
}
```

Summary

Understanding JavaScript is critical to being able to work in the TypeScript and Angular environments. This chapter discusses enough of the basic JavaScript language syntax for you to grasp the concepts in the rest of the book. You've learned how to create objects, how to use functions, and how to work with strings and arrays. You've also learned how to apply error handling to your scripts.

Jumping into TypeScript

Angular is built on TypeScript, so it is important that you have an understanding of it in order to use Angular. This chapter will help you understand the fundamentals of TypeScript.

This chapter will familiarize you with the additions TypeScript gives to JavaScript. If you are familiar with C# and object-oriented programming, TypeScript will seem more familiar than JavaScript. This chapter will also familiarize you with the basics of programming in TypeScript; it discusses types, interfaces, classes, modules, functions, and generics. Like Chapter 1, "Jumping into JavaScript," it is not intended to be a full language guide; rather, it is a primer on the language to help prepare you for using Angular.

Learning the Different Types

Like JavaScript, TypeScript uses data types to handle data, but there are some differences in syntax. TypeScript also adds in an extra type enumeration. The following list goes over the types and variables and their syntax for TypeScript:

- **String:** This data type stores character data as a string. The character data is specified by either single or double quotation marks. All the data contained in the quotes will be assigned to the string variable. Consider these examples:

```
var myString: string = 'Some Text';
var anotherString: string = "Some More Text";
```

- **Number:** This data type stores data as a numeric value. Numbers are useful in counting, calculations, and comparisons. Here are some examples:

```
var myInteger: number = 1;
var cost: number = 1.33;
```

- **Boolean:** This data type stores a single bit that is either `true` or `false`. Booleans are often used for flags. For example, you might set a variable to `false` at the beginning of some code and then check it on completion to see if the code execution hit a certain spot. The following examples define `true` and `false` variables:

```
var yes: boolean = true;
var no: boolean = false;
```

- **Array:** An indexed array is a series of separate distinct data items, all stored under a single variable name. Items in the array can be accessed by their zero-based index, using `array[index]`. The following are two examples of creating a simple array and then accessing the first element, which is at index `0`:

```
var arr:string[] = ["one", "two", "three"];
var firstInArr = arr[0];
var arr2:Array<number> = ["a", "second", "array"];
var firstInArr2 = arr[0];
```

- **Null:** Sometimes you do not have a value to store in a variable either because it hasn't been created or you are no longer using it. At such a time, you can set a variable to `null`. Using `null` is better than assigning a value of `0` or an empty string (`""`) because those may be valid values for the variable. By assigning `null` to a variable, you can assign no value and check against `null` inside your code, like this:

```
var newVar = null;
```

- **Any:** In TypeScript you may not always know what type of variable you will be getting or using. In such a case, you can assign the variable type as `any` to allow any other type to be assigned to a variable. The following is an example of assigning multiple types to the same variable:

```
Var anyType: any = "String Assigned";
Var anyType = 404;
Var anyType = True;
```

- **Void:** You use void when you don't want a variable to have any type at all. In TypeScript using `void` prohibits you from assigning or returning a value. In most cases you use `void` when declaring a function you don't want to have a return value. The following example is a function of type `void`:

```
function empty(): void { document.write("code goes here"); }
```

- **Enum:** TypeScript lets us use `enum`, which allows you to give names to enumerated values. The following is the syntax to declare `enum`:

```
Enum People {Bob, John, Alex}
```

Also, to reference the values in `enum`, you use this syntax:

```
var x = People.Bob
```

or this:

```
var y = People[0]
```

By using this syntax, you set `var` x equal to the number `0` and `var` y equal to the string `Bob`.

Understanding Interfaces

Interfaces are a fundamental part of TypeScript. They allow you to have a set structure for an application. They are powerful tools that allow you to set structures for objects, functions, arrays, and classes. You can think of interfaces as defining standards you want your interface subsets to follow.

To define an interface in TypeScript, you use the keyword `interface` followed by the structure you want your objects to follow, like this:

```
interface Person {
    hairColor: string;
    age: number;
}
```

You can also add optional items to interfaces to allow some flexibility within a program. You do this by using the syntax `attribute?: Boolean;`, as shown in the following examples:

```
interface Person {
    hairColor: string;
    age: number;
    alive?: Boolean;
}
```

You can define an interface for functions in TypeScript. This helps ensure that functions take in specific types of parameters. The following example sets `var z` equal to `variables x + y,` using an instance of the interface `AddNums`:

```
interface AddNums {
    (num1: number, num2: number)
}
var x: number = 5;
var y: number = 10;

var newNum: AddNums;
newNum = function(num1: number, num2: number){
    var result: number = num1 + num2;
    document.write(result)
    return result;
}

var z = newNum(x, y);
```

Interfaces also allow you to define how you would like arrays to look. You give arrays the index type to define the types allowed for an object's index. You then give the return type for the index. Here is an example:

```
interface Stringy {
    [index: number]: string;
}
```

```
var coolArray: Stringy;
coolArray = ["Apples", "Bananas"];
```

Finally, interfaces allow you to define class structures. As with a function interface, this allows you to set required variables and methods within each class. It's important to note that this only describes the public portion of a class and not a private section. (We talk more about classes in the next section.) In this example, the interface has a property called name and a method called feed:

```
interface PersonInterface {
    name: string;
    feed();
}
```

Implementing Classes

JavaScript is a language that is based on prototype inheritance. Thanks to ECMAScript 6 (ES6) and TypeScript, you can use class-based programming. You can describe the objects you put into a program by using the base attributes to describe classes.

To define a class in TypeScript, you use the syntax class ClassName{ code goes here }. The following example defines a simple class that defines a Person object with a feed function:

```
class Person {
    name: string;
    age: number;
    hungry: boolean = true;
    constructor(name: string, age?: number) {
        this.name = name;
        this.age = age;
    }
    feed() {
        this.hungry = false;
        return "Yummy!";
    }
}
var Brendan = new Person("Brendan", 21);
```

Notice that the last line uses the new keyword to call into the constructor and initiate a new instance of the class with the name Brendan. This uses the constructor method from the class, which pulls in "Brendan" and 21 as its parameters to build a person named Brendan.

Say that you have a method feed as part of your class that you would like to be able to use. Here is how you use it:

```
Brendan.feed()
```

Class **Inheritance**

Classes are subject to inheritance, and you can pass functionality to other classes by using methods and attributes. This example shows how you can make an extension of Person called SecretAgent and give it extra properties that Person doesn't have:

```
class SecretAgent extends Person {
    licenseToKill: boolean = true;
    weaponLoaded: boolean = true;
    unloadWeapon() {
        this.weaponLoaded = false;
        return "clip empty";
    }
    loadWeapon() {
        this.weaponLoaded = true;
        return "locked 'n' loaded";
    }
}

var doubleOSeven = new SecretAgent("James Bond");
let loadResult = doubleOSeven.loadWeapon();
let unloadResult = doubleOSeven.unloadWeapon();
let feedResult = doubleOSeven.feed();
```

So now you have a class SecretAgent that extends the Person class. This means you can still invoke the original feed method on the Person class, but it gives you some extra attributes and methods on the SecretAgent class.

Implementing Modules

Modules in TypeScript allow you to organize your code over multiple files. This helps keep your files shorter and more maintainable. Modules are able to do this by allowing you to import the functionality you need from within the module you are working on. You can do this if you export the class you need functionality from.

The following example splits the Person class into two separate modules:

```
module Person {
    export interface PersonInterface {
        name: string;
        hungry: boolean;
        feed();
    }
}

/// <reference path="Person.ts" />
module Person {
    export class Person implements PersonInterface {
    name: string;
```

```
    age: number;
    hungry: boolean = true;
    constructor(name: string, age?: number) {
        this.name = name;
        this.age = age;
    }
    feed() {
        this.hungry = false;
        return 'Yummy!';
    }
    }
}
```

```
var Brendan = newPerson("Brendan", 21);
```

In this example, the root module has the interface for `Person`. The submodule starts by using `/// <reference path="Person.ts" />` to point to the root module so it can have access to the `PersonInterface` interface. The example then proceeds to build the `Person` class in the submodule.

Understanding Functions

Functions in TypeScript are similar to functions in JavaScript, but they have added capabilities. TypeScript functions allow you to give types to the parameters and even to what will be returned by a function. While giving a function a type is optional, it's very helpful when you want to make sure that your functions don't give you back something you don't want.

TypeScript allows you to give a function a return type, much in the same way you give return types to variables. You first declare the function name and parameters, and then you can define the type of the function. Also remember that you can assign types to the parameters as well. Check out the following example:

```
function hello(x: string, y: string): string{
    Return x + ' ' + y;
}
```

Like interfaces, TypeScript functions give you the power to create optional parameters. This is helpful when you know that parameters may be circumstantial. It's important to know that optional parameters need to come after the required ones, or an error will be thrown. The following example shows a function `soldierOfGondor` which takes in a required variable name, and an optional variable `prefWeapon`:

```
function soldierOfGondor(name: string, prefWeapon?: string){
    Return "Welcome " + name + " to the Gondor infantry."
}
```

With TypeScript functions, you can create default parameters. A default parameter is optional, but if it isn't given, it has a default value instead of nothing. You create a default parameter by setting one of the parameters equal to the desired default value:

```
function soldierOfGondor(name: string, prefWeapon = "Sword"){
    return "hello " + name + " you can pick up your " + prefWeapon + " at the armory.";
}
```

Summary

Understanding TypeScript is critical to being able to use Angular to its full potential. This chapter goes over enough of the fundamental TypeScript properties and methods to get you through the rest of the book. You've learned how TypeScript uses its different types and how to write and use interfaces, classes, modules, and functions.

3

Getting Started with Angular

Angular is a perfect client-side framework for most web applications because it provides a very clean and structured approach. With a clean, structured front end, you will find that it is much easier to implement clean, well-structured server-side logic.

This chapter introduces you to Angular as well as the major components involved in an Angular application. It is critical that you understand these components before you try to implement an Angular application because the framework is different from more traditional JavaScript web application programming.

After you get a good grasp of the components of an Angular application, you'll learn how to construct a basic Angular application, step by step. This should prepare you to jump into the following chapters, which provide much more detail on implementing Angular.

Why Angular?

JavaScript is a powerful programming language that allows developers to use a web browser as a full application platform. Angular provides a great framework that makes it faster and easier to create client-side JavaScript applications. Developers use Angular because it provides a lot of the structure of web applications—such as data binding, dependency injection, and HTTP communications—that teams would otherwise need to develop themselves.

Understanding Angular

Angular is a JavaScript framework, which means it provides a number of APIs and structure that helps you quickly and easily create complex client-side code. Angular does a great job at providing not only features but also a basic framework and programming model to create client applications. The following sections describe the most important aspects of the Angular framework and how they contribute to make Angular a great JavaScript framework.

Modules

In general, Angular apps use a modular design. While not required, modules are highly recommended because they allow you to separate your code into separate files. This helps you keep your code files short and manageable while still allowing you to access the functionality from each one.

Unlike how you use modules with TypeScript, with Angular you import external modules at the top of a file and export the functionality you need at the bottom. You do this by using the key terms `import` and `export`, with the following syntax:

```
Import {Component} from 'angular2/core';
Export class App{}
```

Directives

Directives are JavaScript classes with metadata that defines the structure and behavior. Directives provide the majority of UI functionality for Angular applications. There are three major types of directives:

- **Components:** A component directive is a directive that incorporates an HTML template with JavaScript functionality to create a self-contained UI element that can be added to an Angular application as a custom HTML element. Components are likely to be the directives you use the most in Angular.

- **Structural:** You use structural directives when you need to manipulate the DOM. Structural directives allow you to create and destroy elements and components from a view.

- **Attribute:** An attribute directive changes the appearance and behavior of HTML elements by using HTML attributes.

Data Binding

One of the best features of Angular is the built-in *data binding*—the process of linking data from a component with what is displayed in a web page. Angular provides a very clean interface to link model data to elements in a web page.

When data is changed on a web page, the model is updated, and when data is changed in the model, the web page is automatically updated. This way, the model is always the only source for data represented to the user, and the view is just a projection of the model.

Dependency Injection

Dependency injection is a process in which a component defines dependencies on other components. When the code is initialized, the dependent component is made available for access within the component. Angular applications make heavy use of dependency injection.

A common use for dependency injection is consuming services. For example, if you are defining a component that requires access to a web server via HTTP requests, you can inject the

HTTP services into the component, and the functionality is available in the component code. In addition, one Angular component consumes the functionality of another via dependency.

Services

Services are the major workhorses in the Angular environment. Services are singleton classes that provide functionality for a web app. For example, a common task of web applications is to perform AJAX requests to a web server. Angular provides an HTTP service that houses all the functionality to access a web server.

The service functionality is completely independent of context or state, so it can be easily consumed from the components of an application. Angular provides a lot of built-in service components for basic uses, such as HTTP requests, logging, parsing, and animation. You can also create your own services and reuse them throughout your code.

Separation of Responsibilities

An extremely important part of designing Angular applications is the separation of responsibilities. The whole reason you choose a structured framework is to ensure that code is well implemented, easy to follow, maintainable, and testable. Angular provides a very structured framework to work from, but you still need to ensure that you implement Angular in the appropriate manner.

The following are a few rules to follow when implementing Angular:

- The view acts as the official presentation structure for the application. Indicate any presentation logic as directives in the HTML template of the view.

- If you need to perform any DOM manipulation, do it in a built-in or custom directive JavaScript code—and nowhere else.

- Implement any reusable tasks as services and add them to your modules by using dependency injection.

- Ensure that the metadata reflects the current state of the model and is the single source for data consumed by the view.

- Define controllers within the module namespace and not globally to ensure that your application can be packaged easily and avoid overwhelming the global namespace.

Adding Angular to Your Environment

To get started with Angular, you need to set up a few things first to get it ready to use. Here's what you need:

- Angular libraries to make Angular applications

- A web server to serve the files to the browser

- A transpiler to convert your TypeScript code back to JavaScript

- A watcher so that the transpiler knows when there has been a file change

- An editor in which to write your code

> **Note**
>
> We recommend that you use Visual Studio Code (https://code.visualstudio.com/); it has good TypeScript and Angular support built in, and is a light-weight editor with many available extensions.

Fortunately, the Angular team has done most of the work for you here. All you need to do is go to the Angular QuickStart website, which walks you through the process. The following Angular QuickStart website takes you through the basics of Angular: https://angular.io/docs/ts/latest/quickstart.html. This website explains the basics of Angular's command-line interface (CLI): https://angular.io/docs/ts/latest/cli-quickstart.html.

> **Note**
>
> We recommend that you use the CLI while learning Angular. The CLI generates all the bootstrap and configuration files for you. It also includes a lightweight server for testing your code.

Using the Angular CLI

Angular provides a powerful CLI that makes building out Angular applications a much more streamlined process. By using the CLI, you will quickly be able to generate new Angular applications, components, directives, pipes, and services. The following sections go over some of the most important tools available through the CLI.

Generating Content with the CLI

One of the most common purposes of the CLI is to generate content for applications. It automates the process of creating and bootstrapping a new Angular application, letting you get straight to the meat of the application.

From the command line, run the command `ng new [application name]` to create a new Angular application. If you navigate to that newly created application, you have access too many other useful commands. Table 3.1 lists some of the most important commands that the CLI has to offer.

Table 3.1   **Angular CLI Command Options**

Command	Alias	Purpose
`ng new`		Creates a new Angular application
`ng serve`		Builds and runs the angular application for testing
`ng eject`		Makes the webpack config files available to be edited
`ng generate component [name]`	`ng g c [name]`	Creates a new component
`ng generate directive [name]`	`ng g d [name]`	Creates a new directive
`ng generate module [name]`	`ng g m [name]`	Creates a module
`ng generate pipe [name]`	`ng g p [name]`	Creates a pipe
`ng generate service [name]`	`ng g s [name]`	Creates a service
`ng generate enum [name]`	`ng g e [name]`	Creates an enumeration
`ng generate guard [name]`	`ng g g [name]`	Creates a guard
`ng generate interface [name]`	`ng g i [name]`	Creates an interface

While an in-depth guide of everything the CLI has to offer is beyond the scope of this book, it is worth learning how to use.

Creating a Basic Angular Application

Now that you understand the basics of the Angular CLI, you are ready to get started implementing Angular code. This section walks you through a very basic Angular application that implements an Angular component with an inline template, an inline stylesheet, and the Component class.

For this example, it is expected that you have started working through the Angular QuickStart guide and understand the basics of the CLI. The first thing to do is to create a directory where you can place your projects.

When you have your directory set up, the next step is to generate your first Angular application. Run the following command to create the application for this example:

`ng new first`

Next, run the following command to launch a server that will render the application:

`ng serve`

The following sections describe the important steps in implementing the Angular application and the code involved in each step. Each of these steps is described in much more detail in later chapters, so don't get bogged down in them here. What is important at this point is that you understand the process of implementing the HTML, component, class, and bootstrap and generally how they interact with each other.

Figure 3.1 shows the web application you are going to create. It shows a simple message that has been printed out by an Angular component.

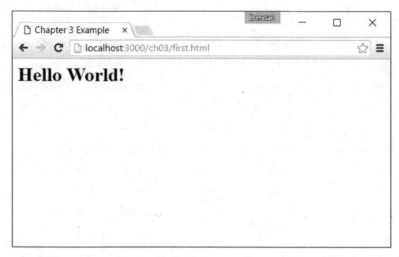

Figure 3.1   Implementing a basic Angular web application that uses a component to load an HTML template to the view

Creating Your First Angular App

Now that you've seen how Angular works, let's get into a practical example. This example doesn't change much that was generated by the CLI, but it will familiarize you with the different pieces of an Angular application.

To get started, navigate to the file `src/app/app.component.ts` in your application directory. It looks like this:

```
01 import {Component} from '@angular/core';
02 @Component({
03   selector: 'message',
04   template: `
05     <h1>Hello World!</h1>
06   `,
07 })
08 export class Chap3Component{
09   title = 'My First Angular App';
10 }
```

Notice that line l imports the component module. Then the component decorator is defined and given a selector and a template. The selector is the name given to the component, and the template is the HTML that the component will generate. For this example, change the template and selector to match the ones on lines 3–6 and change the title variable as shown on line 9.

After the decorator is defined, lines 8–10 create the `export` class to make your component available to the rest of the application as well as define variables and functions that are made available to the component template.

Understanding and Using NgModule

Now that you've created your component, you need some way to tell the rest of your app about it. You do this by importing NgModule from Angular. NgModule is an Angular decorator that allows you to place all your imports, declarations, and bootstrap files for a particular module in a single location. This makes bootstrapping all the files in large applications very easy. NgModule has several metadata options that allow different things to be imported, exported, and bootstrapped:

- `providers`: This is an array of injectable objects that are available in the injector of the current module.

- `declarations`: This is an array of directives, pipes, and/or components that belong in the current module.

- `imports`: This is an array of directives, pipes, and/or components that will be available to other templates within the current module.

- `exports`: This is an array of directives, pipes, and/or modules that can be used within any component that imports the current module.

- `entryComponents`: This is an array of components that will be compiled and will have a component factory created when the current module is defined.

- `bootstrap`: This is an array of components that will be bootstrapped when the current module is bootstrapped.

- `schemas`: This is an array of elements and properties that aren't directives or components.

- `id`: This is a simple string that acts as a unique ID to identify this module.

As is often the case, it's easiest to learn this by doing, so let's get started using `NgModule`. Navigate to the file named `app.module.ts` in your `app` folder. It looks like this:

```
01 import { BrowserModule } from '@angular/platform-browser';
02 import { NgModule } from '@angular/core';
03 import { FormsModule } from '@angular/forms';
04 import { HttpModule } from '@angular/http';
05
06 import { Chap3Component } from './app.component';
07
```

```
08 @NgModule({
09   declarations: [
10     Chap3Component
11   ],
12   imports: [
13     BrowserModule,
14     FormsModule,
15     HttpModule
16   ],
17   providers: [],
18   bootstrap: [Chap3Component]
19 })
20 export class AppModule { }
```

First, you import NgModule, BrowserModule, and any custom components, directives, services, and so on that your app has. Second, you configure the @NgModule object to bootstrap everything together. Notice that when the component is imported, the bootstrap property has the component's export class name. Finally, you export the class named AppModule.

Creating the Angular Bootstrapper

Now that you've looked at your component and module, you need some way to tell the rest of your app about it. You do this by importing the bootstrapper through platformBrowserDynamic from Angular.

Navigate to the file named main.ts in your app folder, which looks like this:

```
01 import { enableProdMode } from '@angular/core';
02 import { platformBrowserDynamic } from '@angular/platform-browser-dynamic';
03
04 import { AppModule } from './app/app.module';
05 import { environment } from './environments/environment';
06
07 if (environment.production) {
08   enableProdMode();
09 }
10
11 platformBrowserDynamic().bootstrapModule(AppModule);
```

The imports are enableProdMode, platformBrowserDynamic, AppModule, and environment. enableProdMode uses Angular's optimizations for a production application. platformBrowserDynamic is used to bootstrap the application together, using the application module AppModule, as shown in the following code:

platformBrowserDynamic().bootstrapModule(AppModule);The environment variable determines the state of the application—whether it should be deployed in development mode or production mode.

platform is then assigned the result from the function platformBrowserDynamic. platform has the method bootstrapModule(), which consumes the module. Notice that when you import and bootstrap a component, the name you use is the same as the component's export class.

Now open the command prompt, navigate to your root directory, and run the command ng serve. This command compiles your code and opens a browser window. You may need to point your browser to the local host and port. The command lets you know the URL to navigate your browser to, as shown in the following example:

```
** NG Live Development Server is running on http://localhost:4200 **
```

Listing 3.1 shows the html index file that loads the application. Line 12 shows where the message component gets applied.

Listing 3.2 shows the Angular module that bootstraps the component. Lines 1–4 show the Angular modules BrowserModule, NgModule, FormsModule, and HttpModule each getting imported. Line 6 shows the Angular component Chap3Component getting imported. Lines 9–11 show the component being declared. Lines 12–16 show the imports array which makes the imported modules available to the application. Line 18 bootstraps the main component of the application.

Note

This application doesn't need the FormsModule, or the HttpModule to run. However, they are included to help show the syntax of importing extra modules into the application.

Listing 3.3 shows the Angular component which has the selector message. This component displays the message Hello World! In the browser.

Listing 3.1   first.html: **A Simple Angular Template That Loads the First Component**

```
01 <!doctype html>
02 <html>
03 <head>
04   <meta charset="utf-8">
05   <title>First</title>
06   <base href="/">
07
08   <meta name="viewport" content="width=device-width, initial-scale=1">
09   <link rel="icon" type="image/x-icon" href="favicon.ico">
10 </head>
11 <body>
12   <message>Loading...</message>
13 </body>
14 </html>
```

Listing 3.2 `app.module.ts`: **An Angular Module that bootstraps the application**

```
01 import { BrowserModule } from '@angular/platform-browser';
02 import { NgModule } from '@angular/core';
03 import { FormsModule } from '@angular/forms';
04 import { HttpModule } from '@angular/http';
05
06 import { Chap3Component } from './app.component';
07
08 @NgModule({
09   declarations: [
10     Chap3Component
11   ],
12   imports: [
13     BrowserModule,
14     FormsModule,
15     HttpModule
16   ],
17   providers: [],
18   bootstrap: [Chap3Component]
19 })
20 export class AppModule { }
```

Listing 3.3 `first.component.ts`: **An Angular Component**

```
01 import {Component} from 'angular2/core';
02 @Component({
03   selector: 'message',
04   template: `
05     <h1>Hello World!<h1>
06   `,
07   styles:[`
08     h1 {
09       font-weight: bold;
10     }
11   `]
12 })
13 export class Chap3component{
14   title = 'Chapter 3 Example';
15 }
```

Listings 3.4 and 3.5 show the compiled JavaScript code from the TypeScript files in Listings 3.2 and 3.3.

Note

This is the only time we show you the compiled JavaScript files in this book because these are generated automatically for you when the application is compiled and run—and to help keep the book more readable.

Listing 3.4 `app.module.js`: **The JavaScript Version of the Angular Module that bootstraps the application**

```
01 "use strict";
02 var __decorate = (this && this.__decorate) ||
03    function (decorators, target, key, desc) {
04      var c = arguments.length, r = c < 3 ? target :
05        desc === null ? desc = Object.getOwnPropertyDescriptor(target, key) : desc,
d;
06      if (typeof Reflect === "object" && typeof Reflect.decorate === "function")
07        r = Reflect.decorate(decorators, target, key, desc);
08      else for (var i = decorators.length - 1; i >= 0; i--)
09        if (d = decorators[i]) r = (c < 3 ? d(r) : c > 3 ? d(target, key, r)
10          : d(target, key)) || r;
11      return c > 3 && r && Object.defineProperty(target, key, r), r;
12 };
13 exports.__esModule = true;
14 var platform_browser_1 = require("@angular/platform-browser");
15 var core_1 = require("@angular/core");
16 var forms_1 = require("@angular/forms");
17 var http_1 = require("@angular/http");
18 var app_component_1 = require("./app.component");
19 var AppModule = (function () {
20      function AppModule() {
21      }
22      AppModule = __decorate([
23          core_1.NgModule({
24              declarations: [
25                  app_component_1.Chap3Component
26              ],
27              imports: [
28                  platform_browser_1.BrowserModule,
29                  forms_1.FormsModule,
30                  http_1.HttpModule
31              ],
32              providers: [],
33              bootstrap: [app_component_1.Chap3Component]
34          })
35      ], AppModule);
36      return AppModule;
37 }());
38 exports.AppModule = AppModule;
```

Listing 3.5 `first.component.js`: **The JavaScript Version of the Angular Component File**

```
01 "use strict";
02 var __decorate = (this && this.__decorate)
03     || function (decorators, target, key, desc) {
04     var c = arguments.length, r = c < 3
05         ? target : desc === null
06         ? desc = Object.getOwnPropertyDescriptor(target, key) : desc, d;
07     if (typeof Reflect === "object" && typeof Reflect.decorate === "function")
08         r = Reflect.decorate(decorators, target, key, desc);
09     else for (var i = decorators.length - 1; i >= 0; i--)
10         if (d = decorators[i]) r = (c < 3 ? d(r) : c > 3
11             ? d(target, key, r) : d(target, key)) || r;
12     return c > 3 && r && Object.defineProperty(target, key, r), r;
13 };
14 exports.__esModule = true;
15 var core_1 = require("@angular/core");
16 var Chap3Component = (function () {
17     function Chap3Component() {
18         this.title = 'Chapter 3 Example';
19     }
20     Chap3Component = __decorate([
21         core_1.Component({
22             selector: 'message',
23             template: "\n    <h1>Hello World!<h1>\n    "
24         })
25     ], Chap3Component);
26     return Chap3Component;
27 }());
28 exports.Chap3Component = Chap3Component;
```

Summary

The Angular framework provides a very structured method for creating websites and web applications. Angular structures a web application using a very clean, componentized approach. Angular uses data binding to ensure that there is only one source of data. It also takes advantage of templates with directives that extend HTML capabilities, enabling you to implement totally customized HTML components.

This chapter looks at the different components in an Angular application and how they interact with each other. At the end of this chapter, a detailed example of how to implement a basic Angular application, including a component, a module, and a bootstrapper is seen.

4

Angular Components

Angular components are the building blocks you use to create Angular applications. Angular components allow you to build self-contained UI elements for an application. Components allow you to control how your application looks and functions through TypeScript code and an HTML template. This chapter discusses how to create Angular components using a TypeScript class that defines the look and behavior of UI elements.

Component Configuration

An Angular component consists of two main parts: the definition in the decorator section and the class section, which defines the logic. The decorator section is used to configure the component, including things like the selector name and HTML template. The class section allows you to give the component its logic, data, and event handlers, as well as export it to be used in other TypeScript files.

With these two sections you can create a basic component. The following example shows what a component might look like:

```
Import {Component} from '@angular/core';
@Component({
    selector: 'my-app',
    template: '<p>My Component</p>'
})
Export class AppComponent{
    Title = 'Chapter 1 Example';
}
```

To create a component, you import `Component` from Angular and apply it to a TypeScript class that you can then use to control the look and functionality of the component. Within the `@Component` decorator are several component configuration options you need to understand. The following list includes some of the most important options available:

- `selector`: This option allows you to define the HTML tag name used to add the component to the application via HTML.

- **template**: This option allows you to add inline HTML to define the look of the component. This is for when there won't be very much code to add, and it's helpful for when you don't want extra files.

- **templateUrl**: This option allows you to import an external template file rather than inline HTML. This is helpful for separating a large amount of HTML code out of a component to help with maintainability.

- **styles**: This option allows you to add inline CSS to your component. Use it when only minor style changes are needed.

- **stylesUrls**: This option allows you to import an array of external CSS stylesheet(s). You should use this rather than styles when importing external CSS files.

- **viewProviders**: This is an array of dependency injection providers. It allows you to import and use Angular services that provide application functionality such as HTTP communications.

Defining a Selector

In a component, a selector tells Angular where to apply the component in HTML. You apply Angular a component to HTML by giving it a selector and then using the selector name as a tag name in your HTML file. This makes the functionality of the Angular component available in HTML. The following is an example of a selector:

```
@Component({
    selector: 'angular-rules'
})
```

You can then add the selector to HTML files by using the following syntax:

```
<angular-rules></angular-rules>
```

> **Note**
>
> It's important to note that when defining a selector name, there can't be any white spaces. For example, you can't name a selector `angular rules`, but you can name it `angular-rules` or `angular_rules`.

Building a Template

You use a template to define how an Angular component should look. Templates are written in HTML, but they allow you to include Angular magic to do some pretty cool things. Angular allows for both inline templates and external template files.

You can add a template to the Angular @component decorator. For a single-line template, you can use either single or double quotes to wrap it. For a multiple-line template, you use backquotes (`); you generally find the backquote key in the upper left of your keyboard, on the same key as the tilde symbol (~). Using the backquote is very important as it will break your code if it's not correct. Here is an example of a single-line template compared to a multiple-line template:

```
@Component ({
    selector: 'my-app',
    template: '<h1>Hello World!</h1>'
})
@Component ({
    selector: 'my-app',
    template: `
  <h1>Hello World!</h1>
    `
})
```

> **Note**
>
> For the template and styles configuration options, you need to use the backquote (`` ` ``), generally located on the same key as the tilde symbol (~).

The same principles you use for templates also apply to CSS. You use the keyword `styles` to tell a component about inline styling. The only major difference is that styles takes in an object of strings instead of just one string. The following example shows some inline styling:

```
@Component ({
    selector: 'my-app',
    template: '<p>hello world</p>',
styles: [`
      P {
          color: yellow;
          font-size: 25px;
      }
    `]
})
```

> **Note**
>
> You need to use the backquote key for a multiple-line stylesheet.

Using Inline CSS and HTML in Angular Applications

You've learned how to implement HTML and CSS in an Angular component. This section builds an example based on that knowledge.

In this exercise you will see how Angular components use and include external templates and stylesheets. The purpose of this exercise is to illustrate how this use of templates allows for more readable and manageable code.

The code in Listing 4.1 is the Angular component. Line 1 imports the component necessary to define the component. Lines 3 through 18 define the component. The component has a very simple template, as shown in lines 5 through 7, and some CSS styling in lines 8 through 13 to go with it.

Figure 4.1 shows the finished Angular component rendered.

Listing 4.1 `intro.ts`: **A Simple Angular Template and Styling to Display a** `<span>` **Element**

```
01 import { Component } from '@angular/core';
02
03 @Component({
04   selector: 'app-root',
05   template: `
06     <span>Hello my name is Brendan</span>
07   `,
08   styles:[`
09     span {
10       font-weight: bold;
11       border: 1px ridge blue;
12       padding: 5px;
13     }
14   `]
15 })
16 export class AppComponent {
17   title = 'Chapter 4 Intro';
18 }
```

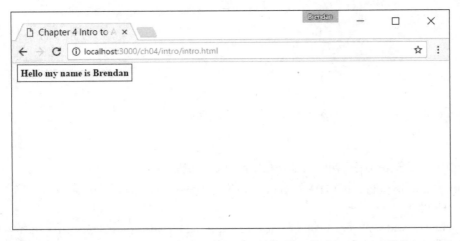

Figure 4.1   Implementing a basic Angular web application that loads an HTML template and styles to the view

Using Constructors

When you use Angular, you often need to have default values and an initial setup for your component variables. Angular uses constructors to give its components default values. This section goes over how to create and implement them.

Constructors go in the `Component` class. Their purpose is to set default values and initial configuration of variables for that class so that when those variables are used within the component, they are never uninitialized. The following is an example of constructor syntax:

```
export class constructor {
    name: string;
    constructor(){
        this.name = "Brendan";
    {
}
```

Now that you've learned what a constructor is and what it looks like, let's get into an example that uses one. This simple exercise uses a constructor to define the current date at the time the component is created.

Listing 4.2 shows an Angular component with a selector named `simple-constructor` and a simple template. Note the `{{today}}` on line 6 is a form of data binding, which is discussed in more detail in Chapter 6, "Data Binding." For now, you should focus on how the constructor works.

Figure 4.2 shows the rendered Angular component.

Listing 4.2   `constructor.component.ts`: **A Simple Component that Displays the Date**

```
01 import {Component} from '@angular/core';
02
03 @Component({
04   selector: 'simple-constructor',
05   template: `
06     <p>Hello today is {{today}}!</p>
07   `,
08 })
09 export class UsingAContstructor {
10   today: Date;
11   constructor() {
12     this.today = new Date();
13   }
14 }
```

Figure 4.2   Implementing a basic Angular web application that uses a constructor to define default variables

Using External Templates

Another way to incorporate templates and stylesheets into Angular components is through a separate file. Using this method is handy because it helps you separate what the files do. It also makes the component easier to read. Under your @Component decorator, you place the keyword templateUrl followed by the path from the root of the application to your template HTML file. Here is an example.

```
@Component ({
    selector: 'my-app',
    templateUrl: "./view.example.html"
})
```

You use the keyword styleUrls to tell the component about external stylesheets. The difference with the external stylesheets is that you pass in an array of one or more stylesheets. The following example shows how to import external stylesheets:

```
@Component ({
    selector: 'my-app',
    templateUrl: "./view.example.html"
styleUrls: ["./styles1.css", "./styles2.css"]
})
```

Note

The styleUrls configuration option takes in an *array* of comma-separated strings.

Earlier in this chapter, in the "Building a Template" section, you learned how to implement external HTML and CSS files into an Angular component. The example in this section builds on that knowledge and walks you through an Angular application that incorporates external HTML and CSS files.

Listing 4.3 shows an Angular component with the selector named `external`, and `templateUrl` and `styleUrls`, which link the external files you need for this application.

Listing 4.4 shows an external template named `externalTemplate.html`. The component uses this file to render the view on the browser.

Listing 4.5 shows an external stylesheet named `external.css`. The component applies this file to the component template file.

Figure 4.3 shows the finished Angular component rendered.

Listing 4.3 `external.component.ts`: **An Angular Component with External File Dependencies**

```
01 import { Component } from '@angular/core';
02
03 @Component({
04   selector: 'app-root',
05   templateUrl: './app.component.html',
06   styleUrls: ['./app.component.css']
07 })
08 export class AppComponent {
09   title = 'Chapter 4 Using External templates and styles';
10 }
```

Listing 4.4 `externalTemplate.html`: **An HTML Template File for the Component to Pull In and Use**

```
01 <h1>Congratulations</h1>
02 <p>
03   You've successfully loaded an external html file.
04   <span>
05     If I'm red then You managed to get the styles in there as well
06   </span>
07 </p>
```

Listing 4.5   `external.css`: **A CSS Stylesheet for the Component to Apply to Its Template**

```
01 span{
02   color: red;
03   border: 2px solid red;
04 }
```

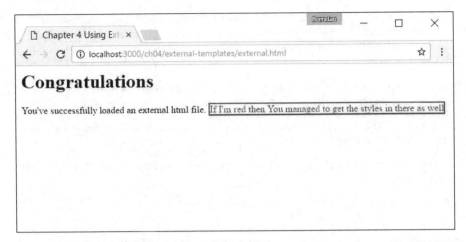

Figure 4.3   Implementing a basic Angular web application that loads an external HTML template and stylesheet to the view

Injecting Directives

Dependency injection can be a difficult concept to fully grasp. However, it is a very important part of Angular, and when you understand the basics, the Angular implementation becomes quite clear. Dependency injection is a well-known design pattern in many server-side languages but had not been used extensively in a JavaScript framework until Angular came along.

The idea of Angular dependency injection is to define and dynamically inject a dependency object into another object, which makes available all the functionality provided by the dependency object. Angular provides dependency injection through the use of providers and an injector service.

In Angular, to use dependency injection on another directive or component, you need to add the directive's or component's class name to the `declarations` metadata in the `@NgModule` decorator within the module for the application, which takes in an array of directives imported into your application. The following is the syntax of the declarations array.

```
...
declarations: [ OuterComponent, InnerComponent ],
...
```

Building a Nested Component with Dependency Injection

You've learned what dependency injection is and how to use it for components and directives. This section shows you how to use what you've learned to create a nested component. This section walks you through an Angular application that incorporates a component that has a second component within it.

Listing 4.6 shows the `outer.component.ts` file, which loads an external template and stylesheet. It also loads and uses the directive `InnerComponent` through dependency injection on line 19. This directive was imported from the `inner.component.ts` file on line 2.

Listing 4.7 shows the `outer.html` template file that the `outer.component.ts` file loads. Notice that the HTML tag `nested` is a custom HTML tag that you use to load the inner component. You do this exactly the same way you load the outer component in the main HTML file.

Listing 4.8 shows the `outer.css` file this gives the outer component and its child components default styles. These styles are inherited by the inner component.

Listing 4.9 shows the `inner.component.ts` file. This is the inner component that the outer component has injected. Notice that the selector for this component, which was used to load this directive within the outer component, is nested.

Figure 4.4 shows the completed application in the browser window.

Listing 4.6   `outer.component.ts`: **The Outer Component for the Application**

```
01 import { Component } from '@angular/core';
02
03 @Component({
04   selector: 'app-root',
05   templateUrl: './app.component.html',
06   styleUrls: ['./app.component.css']
07 })
08 export class AppComponent {
09   title = 'Nested Example';
10 }
```

Listing 4.7   `outer.html`: **An HTML Template for the Component to Apply the View**

```
01 <div>
02   <h1>the below text is a nested component</h1>
03   <nested></nested>
04 </div>
```

Listing 4.8   `outer.css`: **A CSS Stylesheet for the Outer Component to Apply to Its Template**

```
01 div {
02   color: red;
03   border: 3px ridge red;
04   padding: 20px;
05 }
06 nested{
07   font-size: 2em;
08   font-weight: bolder;
09   border: 3px solid blue;
10 }
```

Listing 4.9 `inner.component.ts`: **The Nested Component**

```
01 import {Component} from '@angular/core';
02 @Component({
03   selector: 'nested',
04   template: `
05     <span>Congratulations I'm a nested component</span>
06   `,
07   styles: [`
08     span{
09       color: #228b22;
10     }
11   `]
12 })
13 export class InnerComponent {}
```

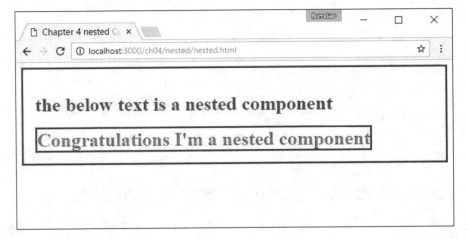

Figure 4.4   Displaying nested components

Passing in Data with Dependency Injection

Dependency injection is a powerful tool that allows you to build a reusable directive to be used within any application that imports that directive. Sometimes data needs to be passed through the application to the directive that's being injected. This is made possible through Angular inputs.

In Angular, to input data to another directive or component, you need to import the `Input` decorator from `@angular/core`. The following code shows the syntax:

```
import {Component, Input} from '@angular/core';
```

When the `Input` decorator has been imported, you can begin to define what data you would like to have input into the directive. Start by defining `@input()`, which takes in a string as a parameter. The HTML uses that string to pass in the data to the imported directive. Do this by using the following syntax:

```
@Input('name') personName: string;
```

Creating an Angular Application that Uses Inputs

Now that you have learned how to use inputs with dependency injection, it's time to get started on an example. This section walks through an Angular application that passes data to a directive from another directive.

Listing 4.10 shows the `person.component.ts` file, which is the entry point for the application that will pass data into the `input.component.ts` file.

Listing 4.11 shows the `input.component.ts` file. It is the component that will take in and handle the inputs from an external directive.

Figure 4.5 shows the completed application in the browser window.

Listing 4.10 `person.component.ts`: **A Component that Imports** `input.component` **and Passes Data to It through the Selector**

```
01 import { Component } from '@angular/core';
02 import {myInput} from './input.component';
03 @Component({
04   selector: 'app-root',
05   template: `
06     <myInput name="Brendan" occupation="Student/Author"></myInput>
07     <myInput name="Brad" occupation="Analyst/Author"></myInput>
08     <myInput name="Caleb" occupation="Student/Author"></myInput>
09     <myInput></myInput>
10   `
11 })
12 export class AppComponent {
13   title = 'Using Inputs in Angular';
14 }
```

Listing 4.11 `input.component.ts`: **A Component that takes Data through Its Selector to Modify What Is Displayed via HTML**

```
01 import {Component, Input} from '@angular/core';
02 @Component ({
03   selector: "myInput",
04   template: `
05     <div>
06       Name: {{personName}}
07       <br />
```

```
08        Job: {{occupation}}
09      </div>
10.   `,
11   styles: [`
12     div {
13       margin: 10px;
14       padding: 15px;
15       border: 3px solid grey;
16     }
17   `]
18 })
19 export class myInputs {
20   @Input('name') personName: string;
21   @Input('occupation') occupation: string;
22   constructor() {
23     this.personName = "John Doe";
24     this.occupation = "Anonymity"
25   }
26 }
```

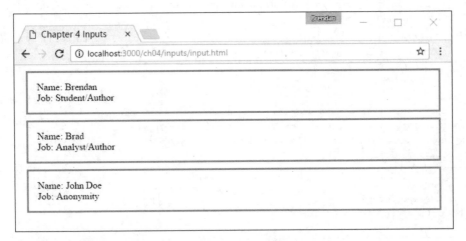

Figure 4.5   Displaying information passed down through inputs

Summary

Angular components are the main building blocks of Angular applications. This chapter shows how to build a component, from the decorator to the class. It shows different ways of including templates and stylesheets. It also shows how to use dependency injection to incorporate external directives or components within each other.

5

Expressions

A great feature of Angular is the capability to add JavaScript-like expressions inside an HTML template. Angular evaluates expressions and then can dynamically add the results to a web page. Expressions are linked to a component, and you can have an expression that utilizes values in the component, and its value can change as the model changes.

Using Expressions

Using expressions is the simplest way to represent data from a component in an Angular view. Expressions are encapsulated blocks of code inside brackets, like this:

```
{{expression}}
```

The Angular compiler compiles an expression into HTML elements so that the results of the expression are displayed. For example, look at the following expressions:

```
{{1+5}}
{{'One' + 'Two'}}
```

Based on these expressions, the web page displays the following values:

```
6
OneTwo
```

Expressions are bound to the data model, which provides two huge benefits. First, you can use the property names and functions that are defined in the component inside your expressions. Second, because the expressions are bound to the component, when data in the component changes, so do the expressions. For example, say that a component contains the following values:

```
name: string='Brad';
score: number=95;
```

You can directly reference the name and score values in the template expressions, as shown here:

```
Name: {{name}}
Score: {{score}}
Adjusted: {{score+5}}
```

Angular expressions are similar to TypeScript/JavaScript expressions in several ways, but they differ in these ways:

- **Attribute evaluation:** Property names are evaluated against the component model instead of against the global JavaScript namespace.

- **More forgiving:** Expressions do not throw exceptions when they encounter undefined or null variable types; instead, they treat them as having no value.

- **No flow control:** Expressions do not allow the following:

  - Assignments (for example, =, +=, -=)
  - The new operator
  - Conditionals
  - Loops
  - Increment and decrement operators (++ and --)

  Also, you cannot throw an error inside an expression

Angular evaluates as expressions the strings used to define the values of directives. This means you can include expression-type syntax within a definition. For example, when you set the value of the ng-click directive in the template, you specify an expression. Inside that expression, you can reference a component variable and use other expression syntax, as shown here:

```
<span ng-click="myFunction()"></span>
<span ng-click="myFunction(var, 'stringParameter')"></span>
<span ng-click="myFunction(5*var)"></span>
```

Because the Angular template expressions have access to the component, you can also make changes to the component inside the Angular expression. For example, this (click) directive changes the value of msg inside the component model:

```
<span (click)="msg='clicked'"></span>
```

The following sections take you through some examples of using the expression capability in Angular.

Using Basic Expressions

In this section, you get a chance to see how Angular expressions handle rendering of strings and numbers. This example illustrates how Angular evaluates expressions that contain strings and numbers as well as basic mathematical operators.

Listing 5.1 shows an Angular component. This component has a template that contains several types of expressions wrapped in double curly brackets ({ { } }). Some of the expressions are just numbers or strings, some include the + operation to combine strings and/or numbers, and one applies a === operator to compare two numbers.

Figure 5.1 shows the rendered web page. Note that numbers and strings are rendered directly to the final view. Adding strings and numbers together enables you to build text strings that are rendered to the view. Also note that using a comparison operator renders the word `true` or `false` to the view.

Listing 5.1 `basicExpressions.component.ts`: **Basic Strings and Numbers with Simple Math Operations in an Angular Template**

```
01 import { Component } from '@angular/core';
02
03 @Component({
04   selector: 'app-root',
05   template: `
06     <h1>Expressions</h1>
07     Number:<br>
08     {{5}}<hr>
09     String:<br>
10     {{'My String'}}<hr>
11     Adding two strings together:<br>
12     {{'String1' + ' ' + 'String2'}}<hr>
13     Adding two numbers together:<br>
14     {{5+5}}<hr>
15     Adding strings and numbers together:<br>
16     {{5 + '+' + 5 + '='}}{{5+5}}<hr>
17     Comparing two numbers with each other:<br>
18     {{5===5}}<hr>
19   `,
20 })
21 export class AppComponent {}
```

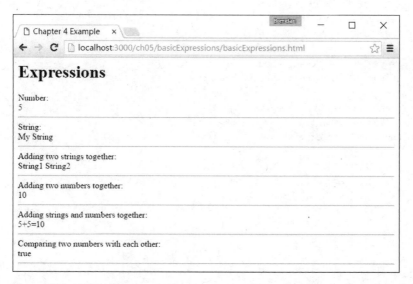

Figure 5.1   Using Angular expressions that contain strings, numbers, and basic math operations

Interacting with the Component Class in Expressions

Now that you have seen some basic Angular expressions, let's take a look at how to interact with the Component class inside Angular expressions. In the previous example, all the input for the expressions came from explicit strings or numbers. This section illustrates the true power of Angular expressions that come from interacting with the model.

Listing 5.2 shows an Angular component file that applies Angular expressions that use values from the Component class to render text to the screen as well as act as parameters to functions. Note that the variable names in the Component class can be used directly in the expressions. For example, the expression in line 9 creates a string based on the values of the speed and vehicle variables.

Figure 5.2 shows the rendered web page, based on the expressions. Note that when the links of the page are clicked, the resulting function calls adjust the Component class variables, which changes how the previously discussed expressions are rendered.

Listing 5.2 `classExpressions.component.ts`: **An Angular Application that Uses Expressions to Interact with Data from the** Component **Class**

```
01 import { Component } from '@angular/core';
02
03 @Component({
04   selector: 'app-root',
05   template: `
06     Directly accessing variables in the component:<br>
07       {{speed}} {{vehicle}}<hr>
08     Adding variables in the component:<br>
09       {{speed + ' ' + vehicle}}<hr>
10     Calling function in the component:<br>
11       {{lower(speed)}} {{upper('Jeep')}}<hr>
12     <a (click)="setValues('Fast', newVehicle)">
13       Click to change to Fast {{newVehicle}}</a><hr>
14     <a (click)="setValues(newSpeed, 'Rocket')">
15       Click to change to {{newSpeed}} Rocket</a><hr>
16     <a (click)="vehicle='Car'">
17       Click to change the vehicle to a Car</a><hr>
18     <a (click)="vehicle='Enhanced ' + vehicle">
19       Click to Enhance Vehicle</a><hr>
20   `,
21   styles:[`
22     a{color: blue; text-decoration: underline; cursor: pointer}
23   `]
24 })
```

```
25 export class AppComponent {
26   speed = 'Slow';
27   vehicle = 'Train';
28   newSpeed = 'Hypersonic';
29   newVehicle = 'Plane';
30   upper = function(str: any){
31     str = str.toUpperCase();
32     return str;
33   }
34   lower = function(str: any){
35     return str.toLowerCase();
36   }
37   setValues = function(speed: any, vehicle: any){
38     this.speed = speed;
39     this.vehicle = vehicle;
40   }
41 }
```

Using TypeScript in Angular Expressions

This section takes a look at some additional TypeScript interactions within the Component class. As described previously, much of the TypeScript functionality is supported in Angular expressions. To illustrate this better, the example in this example shows some array manipulation and uses the TypeScript Math object within expressions.

Listing 5.3 implements an Angular component that uses Angular expressions that take advantage of push() and shift() to display the arrays, show the array length, and manipulate the array elements. Note that with Math added to the Component class, you are able to use TypeScript Math operations directly in the expressions in lines 12 and 21.

Figure 5.3 shows the Angular web page rendered. Notice that as the links are clicked, the arrays are adjusted and the expressions are reevaluated.

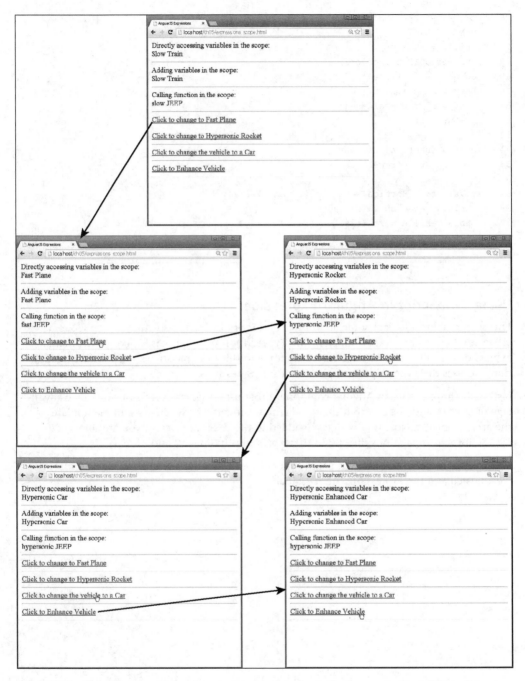

Figure 5.2   Using Angular expressions to represent and use `Component` class data in the
Angular view

Listing 5.3 `typescriptExpressions.component.ts`: **An Angular Component that Uses Expressions Containing Arrays and** `Math`

```
01 import { Component } from '@angular/core';
02
03 @Component({
04   selector: 'app-root',
05   template: `
06     <h1>Expressions</h1>
07     Array:<br>
08       {{myArr.join(', ')}}<br/>
09       <hr>
10     Elements removed from array:<br>
11       {{removedArr.join(', ')}}<hr>
12     <a (click)="myArr.push(myMath.floor(myMath.random()*100+1))">
13       Click to append a value to the array
14     </a><hr>
15     <a (click)="removedArr.push(myArr.shift())">
16       Click to remove the first value from the array
17     </a><hr>
18     Size of Array:<br>
19       {{myArr.length}}<hr>
20     Max number removed from the array:<br>
21       {{myMath.max.apply(myMath, removedArr)}}<hr>
22   `,
23   styles: [`
24     a {
25       color: blue;
26       cursor: pointer;
27     }
28   `],
29 })
30 export class AppComponent {
31   myMath = Math;
32   myArr: number[] = [1];
33   removedArr: number[] = [0];
34 }
```

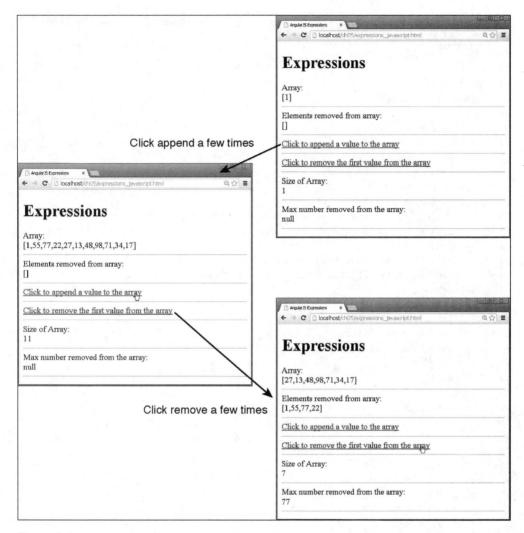

Figure 5.3 Using Angular expressions that apply TypeScript array and Math operations to interact with scope data

Using Pipes

A great feature of Angular is the capability to implement pipes. A *pipe* is a type of operator that hooks into the expression parser and modifies the results of the expression for display in a view—for example, to format time or currency values.

You implement pipes inside expressions, using the following syntax:

```
{{ expression | pipe}}
```

If you chain multiple pipes together, they are executed in the order in which you specify them:

{{ expression | pipe | pipe }}

Some filters allow you to provide input in the form of function parameters. You add these parameters by using the following syntax:

{{ expression | pipe:parameter1:parameter2 }}

Using Built-in Pipes

Angular provides several types of pipes that enable you to easily format strings, objects, and arrays in component templates. Table 5.1 lists the built-in pipes provided with Angular.

Table 5.1   **Pipes That Modify Expressions in Angular Component Templates**

Filter	Description
currency[:currencyCode?[:symbolDisplay?[:digits?]]]	Formats a number as currency, based on the currencyCode value provided. If no currencyCode value is provided, the default code for the locale is used. Here is an example: {{123.46 | currency:"USD" }}
json	Formats a TypeScript object into a JSON string. Here is an example: {{ {'name':'Brad'} | json }}
slice:start:end	Limits the data represented in the expression by the indexed amount. If the expression is a string, it is limited in the number of characters. If the result of the expression is an array, it is limited in the number of elements. Consider these examples: {{ "Fuzzy Wuzzy" | slice:1:9 }} {{ ['a','b','c','d'] | slice:0:2 }}
lowercase	Outputs the result of the expression as lowercase.
uppercase	Outputs the result of the expression as uppercase.
number[:pre.post-postEnd]	Formats the number as text. If a pre parameter is specified, the number of whole numbers is limited to that size. If post-postEnd is specified, the number of decimal places displayed is limited to that range or size. Consider these examples: {{ 123.4567 | number:1.2-3 }} {{ 123.4567 | number:1.3 }}

Filter	Description
date[:*format*]	Formats a TypeScript date object, a timestamp, or an ISO 8601 date string, using the *format* parameter. Here is an example:
	`{{1389323623006	date:'yyyy-MM-dd HH:mm:ss Z'}}`
	The *format* parameter uses the following date formatting characters:
	■ **yyyy:** Four-digit year
	■ **yy:** Two-digit year
	■ **MMMM:** Month in year, `January` through `December`
	■ **MMM:** Month in year, `Jan` through `Dec`
	■ **MM:** Month in year, padded, `01` through `12`
	■ **M:** Month in year, `1` through `12`
	■ **dd:** Day in month, padded, `01` through `31`
	■ **d:** Day in month, `1` through `31`
	■ **EEEE:** Day in week, `Sunday` through `Saturday`
	■ **EEE:** Day in Week, `Sun` through `Sat`
	■ **HH:** Hour in day, padded, `00` through `23`
	■ **H:** Hour in day, `0` through `23`
	■ **hh** or **jj:** Hour in a.m./p.m., padded, `01` through `12`
	■ **h** or **j:** Hour in a.m./p.m., `1` through `12`
	■ **mm:** Minute in hour, padded, `00` through `59`
	■ **m:** Minute in hour, `0` through `59`
	■ **ss:** Second in minute, padded, `00` through `59`
	■ **s:** Second in minute, `0` through `59`
	■ **.sss** or **,sss:** Millisecond in second, padded, `000`–`999`
	■ **a:** a.m./p.m. marker
	■ **Z:** Four-digit time zone offset, `-1200` through `+1200`
	The *format* string for `date` can also be one of the following predefined names:
	■ **medium:** Same as `'yMMMdHms'`
	■ **short:** same as `'yMdhm'`
	■ **fullDate:** same as `'yMMMMEEEEd'`
	■ **longDate:** same as `'yMMMMd'`
	■ **mediumDate:** same as `'yMMMd'`
	■ **shortDate:** same as `'yMd'`
	■ **mediumTime:** same as `'hms'`
	■ **shortTime:** same as `'hm'`
	The format shown here is `en_US`, but the format always matches the locale of the Angular application.
async	Waits for a promise and returns the most recent value received. It then updates the view.

Using Built-in Pipes

This section shows how the built-in Angular pipes handle the transformation of data in Angular expressions. The purpose of this example is to show how pipes transform the data provided.

Listing 5.4 shows the Angular component with a template that contains several examples of built-in pipes wrapped in {{}} brackets. The Component class contains data for some of the pipes to use.

Figure 5.4 shows the rendered application with the transformed data.

Listing 5.4 `builtInPipes.component.ts`: **An Angular Component That Contains an Example of Built-in Pipes**

```
01 import { Component } from '@angular/core';
02
03 @Component({
04   selector: 'app-root',
05   template: `
06     Uppercase: {{"Brendan" | uppercase }}<br>
07     Lowercase: {{"HELLO WORLD" | lowercase}}<br>
08     Date: {{ today | date:'yMMMMEEEEhmsz'}}<br>
09     Date: {{today | date:'mediumDate'}}<br>
10     Date: {{today | date: 'shortTime'}}<br>
11     Number: {{3.1415927 | number:'2.1-5'}}<br>
12     Number: {{28 | number:'2.3'}}<br>
13     Currency: {{125.257 | currency:'USD':true: '1.2-2'}}<br>
14     Currency: {{2158.925 | currency}}<br>
15     Json: {{jsonObject | json}}<br>
16     PercentPipe: {{.8888 | percent: '2.2'}}<br>
17     SlicePipe: {{"hello world" | slice:0:8}}<br>
18     SlicePipe: {{days | slice:1:6}}<br>
19     legen... {{wait | async}} {{dairy | async}}
20   `
21 })
22 export class AppComponent {
23   today = Date.now();
24   jsonObject = [{title: "mytitle"}, {title: "Programmer"}];
25   days=['Sunday', 'Monday', 'Tuesday', 'Wednesday',
26         'Thursday', 'Friday', 'Saturday'];
27   wait = new Promise<string>((res, err) => {
28     setTimeout(function () {
29       res('wait for it...');
30     },1000);
31   });
```

```
32   dairy = new Promise<string>((res, err) => {
33     setTimeout(function() {
34       res('dairy');
35     },2000)
36   })
37 }
```

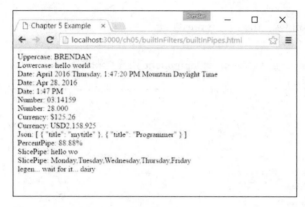

Figure 5.4   Using Angular pipes that transform data within expressions

Building a Custom Pipe

Angular enables you to create your own custom pipes and then use them within expressions and services as if they were built-in pipes. Angular provides the @pipe decorator to create a pipe and register it with the dependency injector server.

The @pipe decorator takes in metadata, just as an Angular component does. The metadata options are name and pure. The name metadata works like the selector of a component: It tells Angular where you want to use the pipe. The pure metadata tells the pipe how to handle change detection. A pure pipe updates when there is a change to the input value or an object reference. An impure pipe can update whenever there is an event, such as a keystroke, mouse click, or mouse movement. The following example demonstrates a sample pipe and its syntax:

```
@Pipe({
    name: 'example',
    Pure: true
})
```

The pipe class works much the same as the Component class, in that it is where the logic of the pipe resides. However, the logic needs to be within a Transform method, which tells the pipe how to transform whatever is to the left of the pipe symbol (|). Review the following example:

```
Export class customPipe{
    Transform(parameter1:string, parameter2:number) : string {
        myStr = "logic goes in here";
        return myStr;
    }
}
```

Creating a Custom Pipe

This section shows how to build a custom pipe that filters out select words from a string. The purpose of this example is to show you how to create and apply a custom pipe that can transform data.

Listing 5.5 shows an Angular pipe with the name metadata censor. The export class contains the Transform method, which replaces certain words with a different string and then returns the transformed string.

Listing 5.6 shows an Angular component which contains template that uses the custom pipe, as well as the pipe metadata to import the pipe. Notice that on line 9, there is the expression that you use to implement the pipe. The pipe takes in a string as an argument and replaces the word with it.

Figure 5.5 shows the rendered application, using the custom pipe.

Listing 5.5   custom.pipe.ts: **An Angular Pipe That Replaces Certain Words in a String**

```
01 import {Pipe} from '@angular/core';
02
03 @Pipe({name: 'censor'})
04 export class censorPipe{
05   transform(input:string, replacement:string) : string {
06     var cWords = ["bad", "rotten", "terrible"];
07     var out = input;
08     for(var i=0; i<cWords.length; i++){
09       out = out.replace(cWords[i], replacement);
10     }
11     return out
12   }
13 }
```

Listing 5.6   customPipes.component.ts: **An Angular Component That Imports and Uses a Custom Pipe**

```
01 import { Component } from '@angular/core';
02
03 @Component({
04   selector: 'app-root',
05   template: `
```

```
06      {{phrase | censor:"*****"}}
07    `
08 })
09 export class AppComponent {
10   phrase:string="This bad phrase is rotten ";
11 }
```

Figure 5.5   Using a custom Angular pipe that transforms data in an expression

Summary

Angular comes with powerful built-in expressions and pipes and provides the option to create custom pipes. This chapter discusses the available built-in expressions and pipes and how to implement them. It also discusses how to build and implement a custom pipe. Expressions are bits of typescript code contained within {{}}, and pipes are able to manipulate those expressions. Expressions have access to information within the Component class and can render class variables to the view.

Data Binding

One of the best features of Angular is the built-in data binding. *Data binding* is the process of linking data from a component with what is displayed in a web page. When data in the component changes, the UI rendered to the user is automatically updated. Angular provides a very clean interface to link the model data to elements in a web page.

Understanding Data Binding

Data binding means linking data in an application with the UI element that is rendered to the user. When data is changed in the model, the web page is automatically updated. This way, the model is always the only source for data represented to the user, and the view is just a projection of the model. The glue that puts the view and the model together is data binding.

There are many ways in Angular to use data binding to make an application look and act in different ways. The following is a list of the types of data binding available with Angular 2 that are discussed in this chapter:

- **Interpolation:** You can use double curly braces ({{}}) to get values directly from the `Component` class.

- **Property binding:** You can use this type of binding to set the property of an HTML element.

- **Event binding:** You can use this type of binding to handle user inputs.

- **Attribute binding:** This type of binding allows the setting of attributes to an HTML element.

- **Class binding:** You can use this type of binding to set CSS class names to the element.

- **Style binding:** You can use this type of binding to create inline CSS styles for the element.

- **Two-way binding with** `ngModel`**:** You can use this type of binding with data entry forms to receive and display data.

Interpolation

Interpolation involves using the {{}} double curly braces to evaluate a template expression. This can be in a hard-coded form, or it can reference a property of the Component class.

The syntax for interpolation should look familiar from Chapter 5, "Expressions." However, you can also use interpolation to give an HTML tag property a value (for example, the img tag). Here is an example of the syntax to do this:

```
<img src="{{imgUrl}}"/>
```

Now let's look at an example that shows some cool things you can do with interpolation binding.

Listing 6.1 shows an Angular component. This component has a template that contains types of interpolation and expressions wrapped in {{}} brackets. The Component class gives values to be used within the {{}} brackets. (Be sure to change the imageSrc variable to the appropriate image name.)

Figure 6.1 shows the rendered web page. As you can see, interpolation can use strings from the Component class to populate the template.

Listing 6.1 `interpolation.component.ts`: **Interpolation with Strings and a Function**

```
01 import { Component } from '@angular/core';
02
03 @Component({
04    selector: 'app-root',
05    template: `
06      {{str1 + ' ' + name}}
07      <br>
08      <img src="{{imageSrc}}" />
09      <br>
10      <p>{{str2 + getLikes(likes)}}</p>
11    `,
12    styles: [`
13      img{
14        width: 300px;
15        height: auto;
16      }
17      p{
18        font-size: 35px;
19        color: darkBlue;
20      }
21    `]
22 })
23 export class AppComponent {
24    str1: string = "Hello my name is"
25    name: string = "Brendan"
26    str2: string = "I like to"
```

```
27   likes: string[] = ['hike', "rappel", "Jeep"]
28   getLikes = function(arr: any){
29     var arrString = arr.join(", ");
30     return " " + arrString
31   }
32   imageSrc: string = "../assets/images/angelsLanding.jpg"
33 }
```

Figure 6.1   Using interpolation to combine strings, define an `imageSrc` URL, and run a function

Property Binding

You use property binding when you need to set the property of an HTML element. You do this by defining the value you want within the `Component` class. Then you bind that value to the component template, using the following syntax:

```
<img [src]="myValue">
```

> **Note**
>
> In many cases, it is possible to use interpolation to achieve the same results you get with property binding.

Now let's take a look at an example of property binding. Listing 6.2 shows an Angular component. This component has a template that contains types of property binding. It also makes a comparison between property binding and interpolation.

Figure 6.2 shows the rendered web page. As you can see, interpolation can use strings from the Component class to populate the template.

Listing 6.2 `property.component.ts`: **Property Binding with Logic and the Application of a Class Name**

```
01 import { Component } from '@angular/core';
02
03 @Component({
04   selector: 'app-root',
05   template: `
06     <img [src]="myPic"/>
07     <br>
08     <button [disabled]="isEnabled">Click me</button><hr>
09     <button disabled="{!isEnabled}">Click me</button><br>
10     <p [ngClass]="className">This is cool stuff</p>
11   `,
12   styles: [`
13     img {
14       height: 100px;
15       width auto;
16     }
17     .myClass {
18       color: red;
19       font-size: 24px;
20     }
21   `]
22 })
23 export class AppComponent {
24   myPic: string = "../assets/images/sunset.JPG";
25   isEnabled: boolean = false;
26   className: string = "myClass";
27 }
```

Figure 6.2   Using property binding to define an `imageSrc` URL, set a button to disabled mode, and assign a class name

Attribute Binding

Attribute binding is similar to property binding but is tied to the HTML attribute rather than the DOM property. You are not likely to use attribute binding very often, but it is important to know what it is and how to use it. You will generally only use attribute binding on attributes that do not have a corresponding DOM property (for example, `aria`, `svg`, and `table span` attributes). You define an attribute binding by using the following syntax:

```
<div [attr.aria-label] = "labelName"></div>
```

> **Note**
>
> Because attribute binding and property binding function almost the same way, we do not present an example for attribute binding in this book.

Class Binding

You use class binding to bind CSS style tags to HTML elements. It assigns the class based on the result of an expression being `true` or `false`. If the result is `true`, the class gets assigned. The following is an example of the syntax:

```
<div [class.nameHere] = "true"></div>
<div [class.anotherName] = "false"></div>
```

Now let's take a look at an example of class binding. Listing 6.3 shows an Angular component that has a template. This template contains types of class binding that show how to apply a class name using two different methods.

Figure 6.3 shows the rendered web page. As you can see, the class names take effect and allow the CSS styles to change the HTML.

Listing 6.3 `class.component.ts`: **Property Binding with Logic and the Application of a Class Name**

```
01 import { Component } from '@angular/core';
02
03 @Component({
04   selector: 'app-root',
05   template: `
06     <div [class]="myCustomClass"></div>
07     <span [class.redText]="isTrue">Hello my blue friend</span>
08   `,
09   styles: [`
10     .blueBox {
11       height: 150px;
12       width: 150px;
13       background-color: blue;
14     }
15     .redText{
16       color: red;
17       font-size: 24px;
18     }
19   `]
20 })
21 export class AppComponent {
22   myCustomClass: string = 'blueBox';
23   isTrue = true;
24 }
```

Figure 6.3 An Angular application that applies class binding to add custom classes to HTML elements

Style Binding

You use style binding to assign inline styles to an HTML element. Style binding works by defining the CSS style property in the brackets, with the assignment expression in the quotation marks. The syntax looks almost the same as for class binding but with `style` instead of `class` as the prefix:

```
<p [style.styleProperty] = "assignment"></p>
<div [style.backgroundColor] = "'green'"></div>
```

Now let's take a look at an example of style binding. Listing 6.4 shows an Angular component that has a template. This template contains types of style binding that show how to apply custom inline styles to an application.

Figure 6.4 shows the rendered web page. As you can see, the styles take effect, and the CSS styles change the HTML accordingly.

Listing 6.4 `style.component.ts`: **Style Binding to Change the Appearance of the HTML**

```
01 import { Component } from '@angular/core';
02
03 @Component({
04    selector: 'app-root',
05    template: `
06      <span [style.border]="myBorder">Hey there</span>
07      <div [style.color]="twoColors ? 'blue' : 'forestgreen'">
08        what color am I
09      </div>
10      <button (click)="changeColor()">click me</button>
11    `
12 })
13 export class AppComponent {
14    twoColors: boolean = true;
15    changeColor = function(){
16      this.twoColors = !this.twoColors;
17    }
18    myBorder = "1px solid black";
19 }
```

Figure 6.4   The rendered web page with custom styles applied via a button that runs a function to adjust the value of the `twoColors` variable

Event Binding

You use event binding to handle user inputs such as clicking, keystrokes, and mouse movements. Angular event binding is similar to HTML event attributes; the major difference is that the prefix on is removed from the binding, and instead the event is surrounded by parentheses (()). For example `onkeyup` in HTML looks like `(keyup)` in Angular.

A common purpose for event binding is to run functions from the component. The following is the syntax for click event binding:

```
<button (click)="myFunction()">button</button>
```

Let's look at an example of event binding. Listing 6.5 shows an Angular component. This component has event binding that calls a function to change the image URL once clicked.

Figure 6.5 shows the rendered web page. You can see both the initial web page and the results of clicking the button to trigger the event.

Listing 6.5 `event.component.ts`: **Event Binding to Change the Image URL That Displays on the Web Page**

```
01 import { Component } from '@angular/core';
02
03 @Component({
04   selector: 'app-root',
05   template: `
06     <div (mousemove)="move($event)">
```

```
07        <img [src]="imageUrl"
08          (mouseenter)="mouseGoesIn()"
09          (mouseleave)="mouseLeft()"
10          (dblclick)="changeImg()" /><br>
11          double click the picture to change it<br>
12          The Mouse has {{mouse}}<hr>
13        <button (click)="changeImg()">Change Picture</button><hr>
14        <input (keyup)="onKeyup($event)"
15          (keydown)="onKeydown($event)"
16          (keypress)="keypress($event)"
17          (blur)="underTheScope($event)"
18          (focus)="underTheScope($event)">
19          {{view}}
20        <p>On key up: {{upValues}}</p>
21        <p>on key down: {{downValues}}</p>
22        <p>on key press: {{keypressValue}}</p>
23        <p (mousemove)="move($event)">
24          x coordinates: {{x}}
25          <br> y coordinates: {{y}}
26        </p>
27      </div>
28    `,
29    styles: [`
30      img {
31        width: auto;
32        height: 300px;
33      }
34    `]
35 })
36 export class AppComponent {
37    counter = 0;
38    mouse: string;
39    upValues: string = '';
40    downValues: string = '';
41    keypressValue: string = "";
42    x: string = "";
43    y: string = '';
44    view: string = '';
45
46    mouseGoesIn = function(){
47      this.mouse = "entered";
48    };
49    mouseLeft = function(){
50      this.mouse = "left";
51    }
52    imageArray: string[] = [
53      "../assets/images/flower.jpg",
54      "../assets/images/lake.jpg", //extensions are case sensitive
```

```
55      "../assets/images/bison.jpg",
56    ]
57    imageUrl: string = this.imageArray[this.counter];
58    changeImg = function(){
59      if(this.counter < this.imageArray.length - 1){
60        this.counter++;
61      }else{
62        this.counter = 0;
63      }
64      this.imageUrl=this.imageArray[this.counter];
65    }
66    onKeyup(event:any){
67      this.upValues = event.key;
68      //this.upValues += event.target.value + ' | ';
69    }
70    onKeydown(event:any){
71      this.downValues = event.key;
72      //this.downValues += event.target.value + " | ";
73    }
74    keypress(event:any){
75      this.keypressValue = event.key;
76      //this.keypressValue += event.target.value + " | ";
77    }
78    move(event:any){
79      this.x = event.clientX;
80      this.y = event.clientY;
81    }
82    underTheScope(event:any){
83      if(event.type == "focus"){
84        this.view = "the text box is focused";
85      }
86      else if(event.type == "blur"){
87        this.view = "the input box is blurred";
88      }
89      console.log(event);
90    }
91  }
```

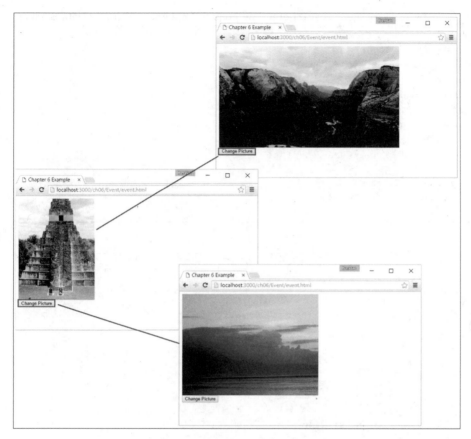

Figure 6.5   The initial result when the web page is loaded and the result from the event being triggered

Two-Way Binding

Two-way binding allows for data to be easily displayed and updated simultaneously. This makes it easy to reflect any changes the user makes to the DOM. Angular does this by using ngModel to watch for changes and then update the value. This is the syntax:

```
<input [(ngModel)] = "myValue">
```

Now let's take a look at an example of two-way binding. Listing 6.6 shows an Angular component that has a template. This template shows different ways to accomplish two-way data binding.

Figure 6.6 shows the rendered web page. It shows that the styles take effect and the CSS styles change the HTML accordingly.

Listing 6.6   `twoWay.component.ts`: **Different Methods to Implement Two-Way Data Binding**

```
01 import { Component } from '@angular/core';
02 @Component({
03   selector: 'app-root',
04   template: `
05     <input [(ngModel)]="text"><br>
06     <input bindon-ngModel="text"><br>
07     <input [value]="text" (input)="text=$event.target.value">
08     <h1>{{text}}</h1>
09   `
10 })
11 export class AppComponent {
12   text: string = "some text here";
13 }
```

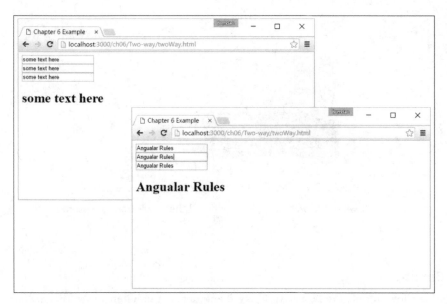

Figure 6.6   An Angular application that shows multiple ways to accomplish two-way data binding. The variable, and the view is updated every time there is a change to the input field

Summary

Angular allows for powerful and very useful types of data binding. As you have seen in this chapter, you can bind data in the application model to the UI elements that are rendered to the user. This chapter goes over the available types of data binding and how to implement them. Data binding allows for data to be both displayed to the user and updated by the user in a simple and efficient manner.

7

Built-in Directives

One of the most powerful features Angular provides is directives. *Directives* extend the behavior of HTML, enabling you to create custom HTML elements, attributes, and classes with functionality specific to an application. Angular provides many built-in directives, which provide the capability to interact with form elements, bind data in a component to the view, and interact with browser events.

This chapter discusses the built-in directives and how to implement them in Angular templates. You will learn how to apply these directives in your Angular templates and support them in back-end controllers to quickly turn a rendered view into an interactive application.

Understanding Directives

Directives are a combination of Angular template markup and supporting TypeScript code. Angular directive markups can be HTML attributes, element names, or CSS classes. The TypeScript directive code defines the template data and behavior of the HTML elements.

The Angular compiler traverses the template DOM and compiles all directives. Then it links the directives by combining a directive with a scope to produce a new live view. The live view contains the DOM elements and functionality defined in the directive.

Using Built-in Directives

Much of the Angular functionality that you need to implement in HTML elements is provided through built-in directives. These directives provide a wide variety of support for Angular applications. The following sections describe most of the Angular directives, which fall into three categories:

- **Component:** A directive with a template
- **Structural:** A directive that manipulates elements in the DOM
- **Attribute:** A directive that manipulates the appearance and behavior of a DOM element.

The following sections describe these three types of directives. You do not need to understand all the directives right away. The following sections provide tables for reference. In addition, the following sections and chapters provide sample code for using many of these directives.

Components Directives

Angular components are a form of structural directive that utilize a template. A component creates a selector that is used as an HTML tag to dynamically add HTML, CSS, and Angular logic to the DOM. Components are at the heart of Angular.

Structural Directives

Several directives dynamically update, create, and remove elements from the DOM. These directives create the layout, look, and feel of an application. Table 7.1 lists these directives and describes the behavior and usage of each.

Table 7.1 **Structural Directives**

Directive	Description
ngFor	This directive is used to create a copy of a template for each item within an iterable object. Here is an example: `<div *ngFor="let person of people"></div>`
ngIf	When this directive is present in an element, that element is added to the DOM if the value returns `true`. If the value returns `false`, then that element is removed from the DOM, preventing that element from using resources. Here is an example: `<div *ngIf="person"></div>`

ngSwitch	This directive displays a template based on the value passed in it. As with `ngIf`, if the value does not match the case, the element is not created. Here is an example:
	
	`<div [ngSwitch]="timeOfDay">`
	`    <span [ngSwitchCase]="'morning'">Morning</span>`
	`    <span [ngSwitchCase]="'afternoon'">Afternoon</span>`
	`    <span [ngSwitchDefault]="'daytime'">Evening</span>`
	
	The `ngSwitch` directive relies on two other directives to work: `ngSwitchCase` and `ngSwitchDefault`. These directives are be explained below.

ngSwitchCase	This directive evaluates the value it has stored against the value passed into `ngSwitch` and determines whether the HTML template it is attached to should be created.
ngSwitchDefault	This directive creates the HTML template if all the above `ngSwitchCase` expressions evaluate to `false`. This ensures that some HTML is generated no matter what.

The directives in Table 7.1 are used in a variety of different ways in various parts of the code. They allow for dynamic manipulation of the DOM, based on what data is passed to them. Structural directives dynamically manipulate the DOM by using expressions or values. Two of the most common structural directives are `ngIf` and `ngSwitch`.

`ngIf` displays a section of HTML if a value or an expression returns `true`. `ngIf` uses the `*` symbol to let Angular know it's there. The following is an example of the syntax for `ngIf`:

```
<div *ngIf="myFunction(val)" >...</div>
<div *ngIf="myValue" >{{myValue}}</div>
```

> **Note**
>
> `ngFor` is another example of a directive that uses the `*` symbol as a prefix to let Angular know it's there.

`ngSwitch` uses `ngSwitchCase`, which displays a section of HTML if a value or an expression returns `true`. `ngSwitch` is surrounded by `[]` as a form of one-way data binding to pass the data to each `ngSwitchCase` for evaluation. The following is an example of the syntax for `ngSwitch`:

```
<div [ngSwitch]="time">
    <span *ngSwitchCase="'night'">It's night time </span>
    <span *ngSwitchDefault>It's day time </span>
```

Listing 7.1 shows an Angular component which has a template that contains built-in structural directives. The `ngIf` directive dynamically adds and removes HTML from the DOM. `ngSwitch` does the same thing as `ngIf`, but it allows for more options, along with a default option if all the cases return `false`.

Lines 6 and 7 in Listing 7.1 use `ngIf` to determine whether the HTML should be displayed.

Line 10 shows the extended form of `ngFor` to dynamically add HTML based on the amount of data passed to it. (This example simply shows another method of using the `ngFor` directive, but the rest of the book will use the shorter form `*ngFor`.)

Line 15 uses the shorthand form of the `ngFor` directive to display data. This method is used throughout the rest of this book.

Lines 20 through 26 use `ngSwitchCase` to determine which piece of HTML should be displayed.

Figure 7.1 shows the rendered web page. As you can see, interpolation can use strings from the `Component` class to populate the template.

Listing 7.1   `structural.component.ts`: **Structural Built-in Functions**

```
01 import { Component } from '@angular/core';
02
03 @Component({
04   selector: 'app-root',
05   template: `
```

```
06    <div *ngIf="condition">condition met</div>
07    <div *ngIf="!condition">condition not met</div>
08    <button (click)="changeCondition()">Change Condition</button>
09    <hr>
10    <template ngFor let-person [ngForOf]="people">
11      <div>name: {{person}}</div>
12    </template>
13    <hr>
14    <h3>Monsters and where they live</h3>
15    <ul *ngFor="let monster of monsters">
16        {{monster.name}}:
17        {{monster.location}}
18    </ul>
19    <hr>
20    <div [ngSwitch]="time">
21      <span *ngSwitchCase="'night'">It's night time
22      <button (click)="changeDay()">change to day</button>
23      </span>
24      <span *ngSwitchDefault>It's day time
25      <button (click)="changeNight()">change to night</button></span>
26    </div>
27    `
28 })
29 export class AppComponent {
30   condition: boolean = true;
31   changeCondition = function(){
32     this.condition = !this.condition;
33   }
34   changeDay = function(){
35     this.time = 'day';
36   }
37   changeNight = function(){
38     this.time = 'night'
39   }
40   people: string[] = [
41     "Andrew", "Dillon", "Philipe", "Susan"
42   ]
43   monsters = [
44     { name: "Nessie",
45       location: "Loch Ness, Scotland" },
46     { name: "Bigfoot",
47       location: "Pacific Northwest, USA" },
48     { name: "Godzilla",
49       location: "Tokyo, sometimes New York" }
50   ]
51   time: string = 'night';
52 }
```

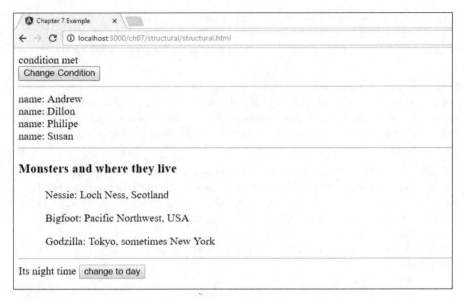

Figure 7.1 Using built-in structural directives

Attribute Directives

Angular attribute directives modify how HTML elements look and behave. They are injected straight into the HTML and dynamically modify how the user interacts with an HTML segment. Attribute directives are so named because they often look like normal HTML attributes. An example of an attribute directive that you've been using throughout the book is ngModel, which modifies an element by changing the display value.

Table 7.2 lists the attribute directives and describes the behavior and usage of each.

Table 7.2 **Attribute Directives**

Directive	Description
ngModel	This directive watches a variable for changes and then updates display values based on those changes. Consider these examples: `<input [(ngModel)]="text"> ` `<h1>{{text}}</h1>`

ngForm	This directive creates a form group and allows it to track the values and validation within that form group. By using ngSubmit, you can pass the form data as an object to the submission event. Here is an example:
	`<form #formName="ngForm" (ngSubmit)="onSubmit(formName)">`
	`</form>`

ngStyle	This directive updates the styles of an HTML element.

The directives in Table 7.2 are used in a variety of different ways in various parts of the code. They allow for manipulation of an application's behavior. The following example shows how to use some of the built-in attribute directives to build a form that submits data to a simulated database.

Listing 7.2 shows an Angular component. Lines 9 through 14 set the default values for the variables used throughout the application. Lines 15 through 17 define the enabler method, which sets the Boolean isDisabled to the opposite value of what it was. Lines 18 through 30 define the addClass method, which pushes a value from the event target to the selectedClass array.

Listing 7.3 shows an Angular template file that uses ngModel, ngClass, ngStyle, and ngForm to modify the look and behavior of the HTML template. Lines 7 through 12 create an HTML selection element that assigns a color to the color variable on the attribute component. Lines 14 through 18 create an HTML selection element that uses the change event to invoke the addClass method and pass in the event object. Lines 16 through 21 display the output of the component variables, using the ngClass and ngStyle directives to dynamically modify the look of the elements.

The code in Listing 7.4 is the CSS for the component that sets up the styles for the application.

Figure 7.2 shows the rendered web page. It shows that interpolation can use strings from the Component class to populate the template.

Listing 7.2 `attribute.component.ts`: **A Component That Builds and Manages an Angular Form**

```
01 import { Component } from '@angular/core';
02
03 @Component({
04   selector: 'app-root',
05   templateUrl: './attribute.component.html',
06   styleUrls: ['./attribute.component.css']
07 })
08 export class AppComponent {
09   colors: string[] = ["red", "blue", "green", "yellow"];;
10   name: string;
11   color: string = 'color';
12   isDisabled: boolean = true;
13   classes:string[] = ['bold', 'italic', 'highlight'];
14   selectedClass:string[] = [];
15   enabler(){
16     this.isDisabled = !this.isDisabled;
17   }
18   addClass(event: any){
19     this.selectedClass = [];
```

```
20      var values = event.target.options;
21      var opt: any;
22
23      for (var i=0, iLen = values.length; i<iLen; i++){
24        opt = values[i];
25
26        if (opt.selected){
27          this.selectedClass.push(opt.text);
28        }
29      }
30    }
31 }
```

Listing 7.3   `attribute.component.html`: **An Angular Template for the Attribute Component**

```html
01 <form>
02   <span>name: </span>
03   <input name="name" [(ngModel)]="name">
04   <br>
05   <span>color:</span>
06   <input type="checkbox" (click)="enabler()">
07   <select #optionColor [(ngModel)]="color" name="color"
08           [disabled]="isDisabled">
09     <option *ngFor="let color of colors" [value]="color">
10       {{color}}
11     </option>
12   </select><hr>
13   <span>Change Class</span><br>
14   <select #classOption multiple name="styles" (change)="addClass($event)">
15     <option *ngFor="let class of classes" [value]="class" >
16       {{class}}
17     </option>
18   </select><br>
19   <span>
20     press and hold control/command
21     <br>
22     to select multiple options
23   </span>
24 </form>
25 <hr>
26 <span>Name: {{name}}</span><br>
27 <span [ngClass]="selectedClass"
28       [ngStyle]="{'color': optionColor.value}">
29 color: {{optionColor.value}}
30 </span><br>
```

Listing 7.4 `attribute.component.css`: **A CSS File That Styles the Application**

```
01 .bold {
02    font-weight: bold;
03 }
04 .italic {
05    font-style: italic;
06 }
07 .highlight {
08    background-color: lightblue;
09 }
```

Figure 7.2   An Angular application that shows multiple ways to apply attribute directives to modify the behavior of the DOM

Summary

Angular offers many built-in directives that provide functionality to manipulate the look, feel, and behavior of an application, without requiring you to write large amounts of code. This chapter goes over some of the available built-in directives and provides examples of how to utilize Angular's built-in directives.

Custom Directives

As with many other features of Angular, you can extend functionality by creating your own custom directives. Custom directives allow you to extend the functionality of HTML by implementing the behavior of elements yourself. If you have code that needs to manipulate the DOM, it should be done inside a custom directive.

You implement a custom directive by calling the @directive class, much the same way you define a component. The @directive class metadata should include the selector of the directive to be used in the HTML. The Directive export class is where the logic for the directive will reside. For example, the following is a basic definition for a directive:

```
import { Directive } from '@angular/core';
@Directive({
    selector: '[myDirective]'
})
export class myDirective { }
```

Creating a Custom Attribute Directive

You can define a limitless number of types of custom directives, which makes Angular incredibly extensible. Custom directives are the most complex portion of Angular to explain. The best way to get you started is to show you an example of custom directives to give you a feel for how they can be implemented and interact with each other.

This section shows how to implement a custom attribute directive. The zoom directive created in this example is designed to add custom functionality to whatever image it is applied to. With this directive applied, you can scroll over an image with the mouse wheel to make the element grow or shrink in size.

Listing 8.1 shows the zoom component, which displays a list of images. These images have the zoom directive applied to them, allowing the mouse scroll event to increase or decrease the size of each image.

Listing 8.2 shows the zoom directive. This directive has the selector zoom. This directive imports Directive, ElementRef, HostListener, Input, and Renderer from @angular/core to provide the functionality this directive needs.

Lines 10 through 12 of Listing 8.2 watch for the mouse cursor to enter the element, and when it does, it applies a border to the element with the `border()` function to let the user know the directive is active.

Lines 14 through 16 remove the border when the cursor leaves the element to tell the user the directive is no longer active.

Lines 17 through 26 listen for the mouse wheel to be activated. Depending on which direction the wheel is scrolled, the element's size is adjusted with the `changeSize()` function.

Lines 27 through 31 define the `border()` function. This function takes in three parameters and then applies those parameters to style the host element.

Lines 32 through 36 define the `changeSize()` function, which changes the size of the host element.

Listing 8.3 shows the HTML file for `zoom.component.ts`. It creates a row of images and applies the zoom directive to those images.

Listing 8.4 shows the styles for `zoom.component.ts`. It sets the height of the images to 200px initially so they aren't rendered huge if they have a high resolution.

The web page that results from Listings 8.1–8.4 is shown in Figure 8.1.

Listing 8.1   `zoom.component.ts`: **A Structural Directive**

```
01 import { Component } from '@angular/core';
02
03 @Component({
04   selector: 'app-root',
05   templateUrl: './app.component.html',
06   styleUrls: ['./app.component.css']
07 })
08 export class AppComponent {
09   images: string[] = [
10     '../assets/images/jump.jpg',
11     '../assets/images/flower2.jpg',
12     '../assets/images/cliff.jpg'
13   ]
14 }
```

Listing 8.2   `zoom.directive.ts`: **A Custom Attribute Directive**

```
01 import { Directive, ElementRef, HostListener, Input, Renderer }
02   from '@angular/core';
03 @Directive({
04     selector: '[zoom]'
05 })
06
```

```
07 export class ZoomDirective {
08     constructor(private el: ElementRef, private renderer: Renderer) { }
09
10     @HostListener('mouseenter') onMouseEnter() {
11         this.border('lime', 'solid', '5px');
12     }
13
14     @HostListener('mouseleave') onMouseLeave() {
15         this.border();
16     }
17     @HostListener('wheel', ['$event']) onWheel(event: any) {
18         event.preventDefault();
19         if(event.deltaY > 0){
20             this.changeSize(-25);
21         }
22         if(event.deltaY < 0){
23             this.changeSize(25);
24         }
25     }
26     private border(
27       color: string = null,
28       type: string = null,
29       width: string = null
30       ){
31         this.renderer.setElementStyle(
32             this.el.nativeElement, 'border-color', color);
33         this.renderer.setElementStyle(
34             this.el.nativeElement, 'border-style', type);
35         this.renderer.setElementStyle(
36             this.el.nativeElement, 'border-width', width);
37     }
38     private changeSize(sizechange: any){
39         let height: any = this.el.nativeElement.offsetHeight;
40         let newHeight: any = height + sizechange;
41         this.renderer.setElementStyle(
42             this.el.nativeElement, 'height', newHeight + 'px');
43     }
44 }
```

Listing 8.3   `app.component.html`: **An HTML File That Uses the Zoom Directive**

```
01 <h1>
02   Attribute Directive
03 </h1>
04 <span *ngFor="let image of images">
05   <img zoom src="{{image}}" />
06 </span>
```

Listing 8.4   `app.component.css`: **A CSS File that Sets the Image Height**

```
01 img {
02   height: 200px;
03 }
```

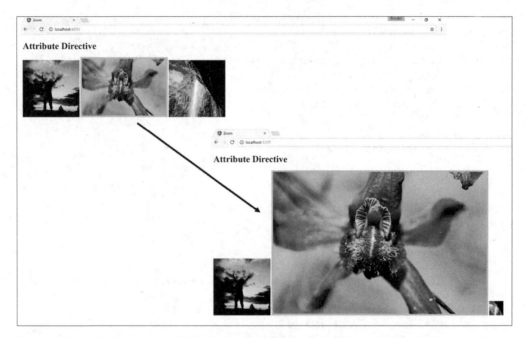

Figure 8.1   Applying a custom attribute directive

Creating a Custom Directive with a Component

Angular components are also a type of directive. What distinguishes a component from a directive is that components use an HTML template to generate a view. But because a component underneath is just a directive, it can be applied to HTML elements to add custom functionality in some really cool ways.

Angular offers a built-in directive called `ng-content`. This directive allows Angular to take existing HTML from between two element tags that use a directive and use that HTML within the components template. The syntax of `ng-content` is as follows:

```
<ng-content></ng-content>
```

The example in this section shows how to use a component as a custom directive to change how the element looks with a containing template.

This example implements a custom directive container that is designed to add a surrounding "container" HTML template to the element it is being applied to. This directive has two inputs title and a description that can be used to give the host element a description and title.

Listing 8.5 shows the root component, which displays various HTML elements. These elements have the container directive applied, which adds a header with an optional title, a footer with an optional description, and borders to each element.

Listing 8.5   `app.component.ts`: **The Root Component**

```
01 import { Component } from '@angular/core';
02
03 @Component({
04   selector: 'app-root',
05   templateUrl: './app.component.html',
06   styleUrls: ['./app.component.css'],
07 })
08 export class AppComponent {
09
10   images: any = [
11     {
12       src: "../assets/images/angelsLanding.jpg",
13       title: "Angels Landing",
14       description: "A natural wonder in Zion National Park Utah, USA"
15     },
16     {
17       src: "../assets/images/pyramid.JPG",
18       title: "Tikal",
19       description: "Mayan Ruins, Tikal Guatemala"
20     },
21     {
22       src: "../assets/images/sunset.JPG"
23     },
24   ]
25 }
```

Listing 8.6 shows the HTML for the root component. The code creates several elements of different types, such as `image`, `div`, and `p`, and applies the container directive to them.

Listing 8.6   `app.component.html`: **HTML for the Root Component**

```
01 <span *ngFor="let image of images" container title="{{image.title}}"
02   description="{{image.description}}">
03   <img src="{{image.src}}" />
04 </span>
05 <span container>
06   <p>Lorem ipsum dolor sit amet, consectetur adipiscing elit,
```

```
07     sed do eiusmod tempor incididunt ut labore </p>
08 </span>
09 <span container>
10    <div class="diver">
11    </div>
12 </span>
```

Listing 8.7 shows the CSS for the root component. It sets a max image height to keep the size of the image smaller. It also sets some default styling for the class diver so that it is visible to the user.

Listing 8.7   `app.component.css`: **CSS for the Root Component**

```
01 img{ height: 300px; }
02 p{ color: red }
03 .diver{
04    background-color: forestgreen;
05    height: 300px;
06    width: 300px;
07 }
```

Listing 8.8 shows the container directive. This directive has the selector `container` and the inputs `title` and `description`. This directive imports `Directive`, `Input`, and `Output` from `@angular/core` to provide the functionality this directive needs. Note that in line 10, ng-content is used to tell the component where to inject the external HTML. Lines 6 through 8 display the passed-in title. Lines 12 through 14 display the description.

Listing 8.8   `container.component.ts`: **A Component that Defines the Container**

```
01 import { Component, Input, Output } from '@angular/core';
02
03 @Component({
04    selector: '[container]',
05    templateUrl: './container.component.html',
06    styleUrls: ['./container.component.css']
07 })
08 export class ContainerComponent {
09    @Input() title: string;
10    @Input() description: string;
11 }
```

Listing 8.9 shows the HTML for the container directive. Lines 2 through 4 create the title bar for the container. Lines 5 through 7 apply the content attribute directive. ng-content acts as a placeholder and will be replaced with the template from the container component shown in Listing 8.8. Lines 8 through 10 create the description bar for the container component.

Listing 8.9   `container.component.html`: **HTML for the Container Component**

```
01 <div class="sticky">
02     <div class="title" >
03          {{ title }}
04     </div>
05     <div class="content">
06          <ng-content></ng-content>
07     </div>
08     <div class="description">
09          {{ description }}
10     </div>
11 </div>
```

Listing 8.10 shows the CSS for the container component. This file sets the CSS to give the container component borders, a title bar, and a description bar.

Listing 8.10   `container.component.css`: **CSS for the Container Component**

```
01 .title {
02     color: white;
03     background-color: dimgrey;
04     padding: 10px;
05 }
06 .content {
07     text-align: center;
08     margin: 0px;
09 }
10 .description {
11     color: red;
12     background-color: lightgray;
13     margin-top: -4px;
14     padding: 10px;
15 }
16 .sticky {
17     display: inline-block;
18     padding: 0px;
19     margin: 15px;
20     border-left: dimgrey 3px solid;
21     border-right: dimgrey 3px solid;
22 }
```

The web page that results from Listings 8.5 through 8.10 is shown in Figure 8.2.

Figure 8.2   Custom component directive

Summary

Angular directives extend the behavior of HTML. Directives can be applied to Angular templates as HTML elements, attributes, and classes. The functionality of directives is defined in the @directive class. Angular provides several built-in directives that interact with form elements, bind data, and interact with browser events. For example ngModel binds the value of a form element directly to the component. When the component value changes, so does the value displayed by the element and vice versa.

One of the most powerful features of Angular is the ability to create your own custom directives. Implementing a custom directive in code is simple, using the @directive class. However, directives can also be very complex because of the myriad ways they can be implemented.

9

Events and Change Detection

Angular has powerful browser events that extend HTML events by using Angular data binding to handle responses. Some of the built-in Angular events are discussed in Chapter 6, "Data Binding," in the section "Event Binding." This chapter goes over built-in events, custom events, and event handling with an Angular application.

Using Browser Events

Using the built-in events in Angular works like data binding. By wrapping an event name in (), you let Angular know what event you're binding to. The event is followed by a statement that can be used to manipulate the data. The following is an example of the syntax for a built-in event:

```
<input type="text" (change)="myEventHandler($event)" />
```

Table 9.1 lists some of the HTML events, along with their Angular counterparts and short descriptions.

Table 9.1   **HTML Events with Angular Syntax and a Description of the Event**

HTML Event	Angular Syntax	Description
onclick	(click)	Event that is fired when the HTML element is clicked on
onchange	(change)	Event that is fired when the value of the HTML element is changed
onfocus	(focus)	Event that is fired when the HTML element is selected
onsubmit	(submit)	Event that is fired when the form is submitted

HTML Event	Angular Syntax	Description
onkeyup, onkeydown, onkeypress	(keyup), (keydown), (keypress)	Events that are fired intermittently when the keyboard keys are pressed
onmouseover	(mouseover)	Event that is fired when the cursor moves over an HTML element

Some of these events should be familiar to you as they have been used in previous chapters. Notice that the Angular syntax uses one-way data binding, which involves using () around each event to pass information about the event to the component.

Emitting Custom Events

A great feature of components is the capability to emit events within the component hierarchy. Events enable you to send notifications to different levels in the application to indicate that the events have occurred. An event can be anything you choose, such as a value changed or a threshold reached. This is extremely useful in many situations, such as for letting child components know that a value has changed in a parent component or vice versa.

Emitting a Custom Event to the Parent Component Hierarchy

To emit an event from a component, you use the EventEmitter class. This class has the emit() method, which sends an event upward through the parent component hierarchy. Any ancestor components that have registered for the event are notified. The emit() method uses the following syntax, where name is the event name and args is zero or more arguments to pass to the event handler functions:

```
@Output() name: EventEmitter<any> = new EventEmitter();
myFunction(){
  this.name.emit(args);
}
```

Handling Custom Events with a Listener

To handle an event that is emitted, you use syntax similar to that used for the built-in events Angular has to offer. The event handler method uses the following syntax, where name is the name of the event to listen for, and event is the values passed by EventEmitter:

```
<div (name)="handlerMethod(event)">
```

Implementing Custom Events in Nested Components

Listings 9.1, 9.2, and 9.3 illustrate the use of EventEmitter, Output, emit, and an event handler to send and handle events up the component hierarchy.

Listing 9.1 shows a custom event component that uses a custom event from a child component to pass data to a variable in the parent. Lines 9 through 11 implement a custom event handler, which takes in an event and applies it to the variable `text`.

In Listing 9.2, line 1 implements a custom event named `myCustomEvent`, which passes the event to the component method `eventHandler`. The `eventHandler` method takes in the emitted value and assigns the value to the variable `text`, which is outputted on line 3.

In Listing 9.3, line 1 imports `Output` and `EventEmitter` from `@angular/core` to be used within the component. Line 15 uses `Output` and `EventEmitter` to create the custom event `myCustomEvent`. Lines 19 and 24 both emit the event and pass the variable `message` to the parent component.

Figure 9.1 shows the rendered web page.

Listing 9.1 `customevent.component.ts`: **A Main Component with an Event Handler**

```
01 import { Component } from '@angular/core';
02
03 @Component({
04   selector: 'app-root',
05   templateUrl: customevent.component.html'
06 })
07 export class AppComponent {
08   text: string = '';
09   eventHandler(event: any){
10     this.text = event;
11   }
12
13 }
```

Listing 9.2 `customevent.component.html`: **HTML That Implements a Custom Event**

```
01 <child (myCustomEvent)="eventHandler($event)"></child>
02 <hr *ngIf="text">
03 {{text}}
```

Listing 9.3 `child.component.ts`: **A Child Component That Emits an Event**

```
01 import { Component, Output, EventEmitter } from '@angular/core';
02
03 @Component({
04   selector: 'child',
05   template: `
06     <button (click)="clicked()" (mouseleave)="mouseleave()">
07       Click Me
```

```
08     </button>
09   `,
10   styleUrls: ['child.component.css']
11 })
12 export class ChildComponent {
13   private message = "";
14
15   @Output() myCustomEvent: EventEmitter<any> = new EventEmitter();
16
17   clicked() {
18     this.message = "You've made a custom event";
19     this.myCustomEvent.emit(this.message);
20   }
21
22   mouseleave(){
23     this.message = "";
24     this.myCustomEvent.emit(this.message);
25   }
26 }
```

Figure 9.1   Creating a custom event

Deleting Data in a Parent Component from a Child Component

Listings 9.4 through 9.9 illustrate the use of EventEmitter, input, Output, emit, and an event handler to send and handle events up the component hierarchy.

Listing 9.4 shows a component that creates a list of characters that can be manipulated via custom events. The selectCharacter() function on line 21 is an event handler that changes the character value, which can then be passed down to the details component.

In Listing 9.5, line 9 implements a custom event called CharacterDeleted, which invokes the deleteChar() method that takes in the event. Lines 24 through 30 of Listing 9.5 implement a handler for the CharacterDeleted event, which removes the character name from the names property. In line 14 of Listing 9.7, the child component emits this event via the emit() method.

In Listing 9.7, line 10 creates the character input, which takes data in from the parent. Line 11 creates the CharacterDeleted EventEmitter, which is used on line 14 to pass the character data back up to the parent to be handled.

In Listing 9.8, line 8 invokes the deleteChar() method which then activates the EventEmitter on line 41 to send the character data back to the parent component.

Figure 9.2 shows the rendered web page.

Listing 9.4   `character.component.ts`: **A Main Component, Which Passes Data Down to a Nested Component**

```
01 import { Component } from '@angular/core';
02
03 @Component({
04   selector: 'app-root',
05   templateUrl: './app.component.html',
06   styleUrls: ['./app.component.css']
07 })
08 export class AppComponent {
09   character = null;
10
11   characters = [{name: 'Frodo', weapon: 'Sting',
12                     race: 'Hobbit'},
13               {name: 'Aragorn', weapon: 'Sword',
14                     race: 'Man'},
15               {name:'Legolas', weapon: 'Bow',
16                     race: 'Elf'},
17               {name: 'Gimli', weapon: 'Axe',
18                     race: 'Dwarf'}
19   ]
20
21   selectCharacter(character){
22     this.character = character;
```

```
23   }
24   deleteChar(event){
25     var index = this.characters.indexOf(event);
26     if(index > -1) {
27       this.characters.splice(index, 1);
28     }
29     this.character = null;
30   }
31
32 }
```

Listing 9.5 `character.component.html`: **HTML That Implements a Custom Event**

```
01 <h2>Custom Events in Nested Components</h2>
02 <div *ngFor="let character of characters">
03   <div class="char" (click)="selectCharacter(character)">
04     {{character.name}}
05   </div>
06 </div>
07 <app-character
08   [character]="character"
09   (CharacterDeleted)="deleteChar($event)">
10 </app-character>
```

Listing 9.6 `character.component.css`: **Styles for the Character Component**

```
01 .char{
02     padding: 5px;
03     border: 2px solid forestgreen;
04     margin: 5px;
05     border-radius: 10px;
06     cursor: pointer;
07 }
08 .char:hover{
09   background-color: lightgrey;
10 }
11 body{
12   text-align: center;
13 }
```

Listing 9.7 `details.component.ts`: **A Details Component That Emits a Delete Event**

```
01 import { Component, Output, Input, EventEmitter } from '@angular/core';
02
03 @Component({
04   selector: 'app-character',
```

```
05    templateUrl: './characters.component.html',
06    styleUrls: ['./characters.component.css']
07  })
08  export class CharacterComponent {
09
10    @Input('character') character: any;
11    @Output() CharacterDeleted  = new EventEmitter<any>();
12
13  deleteChar(){
14    this.CharacterDeleted.emit(this.character);
15  }
16
17  }
```

Listing 9.8   `details.component.html`: **HTML that Triggers a Delete Event**

```
01  <div>
02    <div *ngIf="character">
03      <h2>Character Details</h2>
04      <div class="cInfo">
05        <b>Name: </b>{{character.name}}<br>
06        <b>Race: </b>{{character.race}}<br>
07        <b>Weapon: </b>{{character.weapon}}<br>
08        <button (click)="deleteChar()">Delete</button>
09      </div>
10    </div>
11  </div>
```

Listing 9.9   `details.component.css`: **Styles for the Details Component**

```
01  div{
02      display: block;
03  }
04  .cInfo{
05      border: 1px solid blue;
06      text-align: center;
07      padding: 10px;
08      border-radius: 10px;
09  }
10  h2{
11    text-align: center;
12  }
13  button{
14    cursor: pointer;
15  }
```

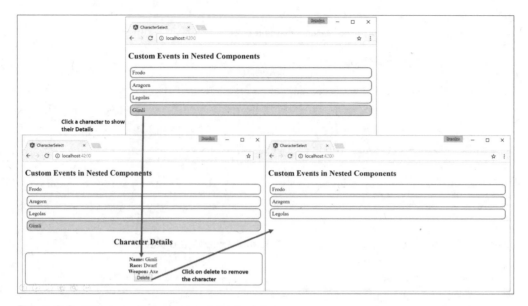

Figure 9.2   Using events to send and delete data

Using Observables

Observables offer components a way to observe data that changes asynchronously, such as data coming from a server or from user input. Basically, observables allow you to watch values for changes over time. Unlike a JavaScript promise, which returns a single value, an observable is capable of returning an array of values. This array of values doesn't have to be received all at once either, which makes observables that much more powerful.

Creating an Observable Object

You import `Observable` from `rxjs/observable` to be used within a component. Once it is imported, you can create an observable object by using the following syntax, where `name` is the observable name:

```
private name: Observable<Array<number>>;
```

Once the observable object is created, it is available to be subscribed to and to make the observable data available to the rest of the component. This is done in two parts: implementing the observable and using the `subscribe` method. This following is a basic example of an observable:

```
01 private name: Observable<Array<number>>;
02 ngOnInit(){
03   this.name = new Observable(observer => {
```

```
04     observer.next("my observable")
05     observer.complete();
06   }
07   Let subscribe = this.name.subscribe(
08     data => { console.log(data) },
09     Error => { errorHandler(Error) },
10     () => { final() }
11   });
12   subscribe.unsubscribe();
13 }
```

Lines 3 through 6 instantiate the observable `name` as `observer`, making it available to be subscribed to. Line 4 uses the method `next` on `observer`, which passes data to the observable. Line 5 uses the method `complete` on `observer` to close the connection of the observable.

The subscription to the observable occurs in lines 7 through 11. This subscription has three callback functions. the first is called when data is successfully received by the subscription. The second is the error handler, which is called when the subscription fails. The third is the final one, which runs code when the subscription completes, whether the subscription succeeds or fails.

On line 8, data is passed to the `console.log` function when the subscription successfully receives the data. Line 9 calls the function `errorHandler`. Line 10 invokes `final()`.

Watching for Data Changes with Observables

Listings 9.10 and 9.11 illustrate the use of `Observable` to watch for changes of data. The example in this section uses observables to watch for data changes and then makes that data available to be displayed on the DOM.

Listing 9.10 shows the component for the application. This component creates two `Observable` objects, `pass` and `run`. These observables have a function that goes and gets a random number between 0 and 30 and gives each number to one of the two teams randomly until the combined total of both teams equals 1,000 or greater.

In Listing 9.10, lines 11 and 12 declare the observables `pass` and `run`. These `Observable` objects are both initialized and subscribed to within the `ngOnInit` function, which runs when the component is initialized.

The observable `pass` is initialized on lines 18 through 20, and `run` is initialized on lines 27 through 28. Once they are initialized, `pass` and `run` both use the function `playLoop` on lines 43 through 52. `playLoop` creates and sends an object that contains a random number between 0 and 1 to determine the team and a random number between 0 and 29 for yards. Each observable then interprets the team and applies the yards to either the team's pass yards or running yards.

Lines 57 through 59 create a random number generator that the rest of the application uses to create the random numbers for the timeout functions, teams, and yards.

Listing 9.11 shows the HTML for this example. This listing has three main parts. Lines 3 through 5 show data for an imaginary team's distance, in yards. Lines 8 through 10 show the same for a second team. Line 11 shows the combination of both teams' distances.

Figure 9.3 shows the rendered web page.

Listing 9.10   `observable.component.ts`: **Observables for Detecting Data Changes**

```
01 import { Component, OnInit } from '@angular/core';
02 import { Observable } from 'rxjs/observable';
03 import { Subscription } from 'rxjs/Subscription';
04 @Component({
05   selector: 'app-root',
06   templateUrl: "./observable.component.html",
07   styleUrls: ['./app.component.css']
08 })
09 export class AppComponent implements OnInit {
10   combinedTotal:number = 0;
11   private pass: Observable<any>;
12   private run: Observable<any>;
13   teams = [];
14   ngOnInit(){
15       this.teams.push({passing:0, running:0, total:0});
16       this.teams.push({passing:0, running:0, total:0});
17       //Passing
18       this.pass = new Observable(observer => {
19         this.playLoop(observer);
20       });
21       this.pass.subscribe(
22         data => {
23           this.teams[data.team].passing += data.yards;
24           this.addTotal(data.team, data.yards);
25       });
26       //Running
27       this.run = new Observable(observer => {
28         this.playLoop(observer);
29       });
30       this.run.subscribe(
31         data => {
32           this.teams[data.team].running += data.yards;
33           this.addTotal(data.team, data.yards);
34       });
```

```
35        //Combined
36        this.pass.subscribe(
37          data => { this.combinedTotal += data.yards;
38        });
39        this.run.subscribe(
40          data => { this.combinedTotal += data.yards;
41        });
42    }
43    playLoop(observer){
44      var time = this.getRandom(500, 2000);
45      setTimeout(() => {
46        observer.next(
47          { team: this.getRandom(0,2),
48            yards: this.getRandom(0,30)});
49        if(this.combinedTotal < 1000){
50          this.playLoop(observer);
51        }
52      }, time);
53    }
54    addTotal(team, yards){
55      this.teams[team].total += yards;
56    }
57    getRandom(min, max) {
58      return Math.floor(Math.random() * (max - min)) + min;
59    }
60 }
```

Listing 9.11 observable.component.html: **A Template File for the Component**

```
01 <div>
02   Team 1 Yards:<br>
03   Passing: {{teams[0].passing}}<br>
04   Running: {{teams[0].running}}<br>
05   Total: {{teams[0].total}}<br>
06   <hr>
07   Team 2 Yards:<br>
08   Passing: {{teams[1].passing}}<br>
09   Running: {{teams[1].running}}<br>
10   Total: {{teams[1].total}}<hr>
11   Combined Total: {{combinedTotal}}
12 </div>
```

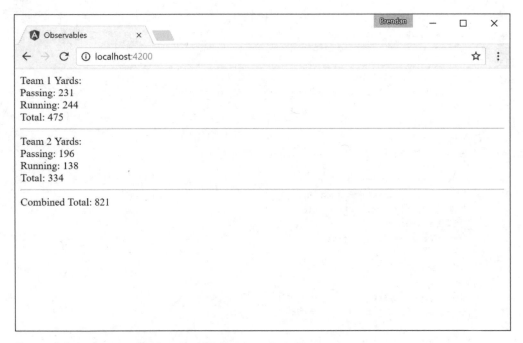

Figure 9.3   Using observables to watch for data changes over time

Summary

The capability to manage events is one of the most critical components in most Angular applications. You can use events in Angular applications to provide user interaction with elements as well as components of the application that communicate with each other so they know when to perform certain tasks.

Components are organized into hierarchies, and the root component is defined at the application level. In this chapter, you have learned how to emit events from within a component and then implement handlers that listen for those events and get executed when they are triggered. You have also learned about observables and how to implement them for asynchronous watching of values.

Implementing Angular Services in Web Applications

One of the most fundamental components of Angular functionality is services. *Services* provide task-based functionality to applications. You can think of a service as a chunk of reusable code that performs one or more related tasks. Angular provides several built-in services and also allows you to create your own customized services.

This chapter introduces built-in Angular services. You will get a chance to see and implement some of the built-in services, such as `http` for web server communication, `router` for managing and changing the state of an application, and `animate` to provide animation capabilities.

Understanding Angular Services

The purpose of a service is to provide a concise bit of code that performs specific tasks. A service does something as simple as providing a value definition or as complex as providing full HTTP communication to a web server.

A service provides a container for reusable functionality that is readily available to Angular applications. Services are defined and registered with the dependency injection mechanism in Angular. This allows you to inject services into modules, components, and other services.

Using the Built-in Services

Angular provides several built-in services that are included in the Angular module, using dependency injection. Once included within a module, services can be used throughout an application.

Table 10.1 describes some of the most common built-in services to give you an idea of what is available. The following sections cover the `http` and `router` services in more detail.

Table 10.1 **Common Services That Are Built in to Angular**

Service	Description
animate	Provides animation hooks to link into both CSS- and JavaScript-based animations
http	Provides a simple-to-use functionality to send HTTP requests to the web server or other service
router	Provides navigation between views and between sections within views
forms	Provides a service that allows for dynamic and reactive forms with simple form validation

Sending HTTP GET and PUT Requests with the http Service

The http service enables you to directly interact with the web server from your Angular code. The http service uses the browser's XMLHttpRequest object underneath but from the context of the Angular framework.

There are two ways to use the http service. The simplest is to use one of the following built-in shortcut methods that correspond to standard HTTP requests:

- delete(url, [options])
- get(url, [options])
- head(url, [options])
- post(url, data, [options])
- put(url, data, [options])
- patch(url, data, [options])

In these methods, the url parameter is the URL of the web request. The optional options parameter is a JavaScript object that specifies the options to use when implementing the request. Table 10.2 lists some the properties you can set in the options parameter.

Table 10.2 **Properties that Can Be Defined in the config Parameter for http Service Requests**

Property	Description
method	An HTTP method, such as GET or POST.
url	The URL of the resource that is being requested.
params	Parameters to be sent. This can be a string in the following format: ?key1=value1&key2=value2&... Or it can be an object, in which case it is turned into a JSON string.

Property	Description
body	Data to be sent as the request message body.
headers	Headers to send with the request. You can specify an object containing the header names to be sent as properties. If a property in the object has a null value, the header is not sent.
withCredentials	A Boolean that, when true, indicates that the withCredentials flag on the XHR object is set.
responseType	The type of response to expect, such as JSON or text.

Configuring the HTTP Request

You can specify a request, a URL, and data by sending the options parameter directly to the http(options) method. For example, the following are exactly the same:

```
http.get('/myUrl');
http({method: 'GET', url:'/myUrl'});
```

Implementing the HTTP Response Callback Functions

When you call a request method by using the http object, you get back an Observable object, which allows the data sent or received to/from the server to be continuously observed. Observables have many operators that use the RxJS library to allow for the transformation and use of the data. The following are some useful methods:

- **map:** Applies a function to each value in the observable sequence. This allows you to dynamically transform the output of the observable stream into custom data formats.

- **toPromise:** Converts the observable into a Promise object, which has access to the methods available on a promise. Promise objects provide syntax to handle asynchronous operations.

- **catch:** Specifies a function to gracefully handle errors in the observable sequence.

- **debounce:** Specifies an interval at which the observable stream will emit values. Only the value of the observable at the interval is emitted; interim values are not emitted.

The following is a simple example of a GET request that returns an observable with syntax to add operators:

```
get(): Observable<any>{
  http.get(url)
    .map(response => response.JSON())
    .catch(err => Rx.Observable.of('the error was: ${err}'));
}
```

Implementing a Simple JSON File and Using the `http` Service to Access It

The code in Listings 10.1 through 10.5 implements a simple mock web server in the form of a JSON file and the Angular application that accesses it. Figure 10.1 shows the output. The web server contains a simple JSON object with a list of users. The web application allows a user to view the list of users. The example is very rudimentary to ensure that the code is easy to follow; it incorporates a GET request as well as an error-handling example.

Listing 10.1 shows the JSON file that contains the JSON object. This file can be accessed using an HTTP GET request, which allows `http` to grab the JSON object and return it to the Angular application as an observable.

Listing 10.1   dummyDB.JSON: **A JSON Object that Contains Data for Users**

```
01 [
02   {
03     "userId": 1,
04     "userName": "brendan",
05     "userEmail": "fake@email.com"
06   },
07   {
08     "userId": 2,
09     "userName": "brad",
10     "userEmail": "email@notreal.com"
11   },
12   {
13     "userId": 3,
14     "userName": "caleb",
15     "userEmail": "dummy@email.com"
16   },
17   {
18     "userId": 4,
19     "userName": "john",
20     "userEmail": "ridiculous@email.com"
21   },
22   {
23     "userId": 5,
24     "userName": "doe",
25     "userEmail": "some@email.com"
26   }
27 ]
```

Listing 10.2 implements the Angular component. `http` is imported on line 3, and `rxjs` is imported on line 5. (Note that you may need to install rxjs via npm.) `rxjs` allows `toPromise()` to be called on the observable object. Notice that the `constructor()` method instantiates `http` on line 15. Line 16 shows an HTTP GET request, which has the path to the dummyDB.JSON file passed in as url. The toPromise() method is called to convert the observable response from the http.get() method into a promise object. Once the promise completes, .then() is called, which takes in the promise object data and applies it to the array users so it can be displayed in the application. If an error occurs, catch is called, which passes the error response object to a callback function to be used.

Listing 10.2 http.component.ts: A Component that Implements the HTTP Service for a GET Request

```
01 import { Component } from '@angular/core';
02 import { Observable }       from 'rxjs/Observable';
03 import { Http }       from '@angular/http';
04
05 import 'rxjs/Rx';
06
07 @Component({
08   selector: 'app-root',
09   templateUrl: './app.component.html',
10   styleUrls: ['./app.component.CSS']
11 })
12 export class AppComponent {
13   users = [];
14
15   constructor(private http: Http){
16       http.get('../assets/dummyDB.JSON')
17         .toPromise()
18         .then((data) => {
19           this.users = data.JSON()
20         })
21         .catch((err) =>{
22           console.log(err);
23         })
24   }
25 }
```

Listing 10.3 implements an Angular module that imports HttpModule to allow the http service to be used throughout the application. HttpModule is imported from @angular/http on line 4 and then added to the imports array on line 15.

Listing 10.3 app.module.ts: An Angular Module that Imports HttpModule for Use in the Application

```
01 import { BrowserModule } from '@angular/platform-browser';
02 import { NgModule } from '@angular/core';
03 import { FormsModule } from '@angular/forms';
04 import { HttpModule } from '@angular/http';
05
```

```
06 import { AppComponent } from './app.component';
07
08 @NgModule({
09   declarations: [
10     AppComponent
11   ],
12   imports: [
13     BrowserModule,
14     FormsModule,
15     HttpModule
16   ],
17   providers: [],
18   bootstrap: [AppComponent]
19 })
20 export class AppModule { }
```

Listing 10.4 implements an Angular template that uses ngFor to create a list of users to be displayed in the application.

Listing 10.4 `http.component.html`: **An Angular Template that Displays a List of Users Received from the Database**

```
01 <h1>
02   Users
03 </h1>
04 <div class="user" *ngFor="let user of users">
05   <div><span>Id:</span> {{user.userId}}</div>
06   <div><span>Username:</span> {{user.userName}}</div>
07   <div><span>Email:</span> {{user.userEmail}}</div>
08 </div>
```

Listing 10.5 is a CSS file that styles the application so that each user is distinguishable from the rest and easy to see.

Listing 10.5 `http.component.CSS`: **A CSS File that Adds Styles to the Application**

```
01 span{
02   width: 75px;
03   text-align: right;
04   font-weight: bold;
05   display: inline-block;
06 }
07 .user{
08   border: 2px ridge blue;
09   margin: 10px 0px;
10   padding: 5px;
11 }
```

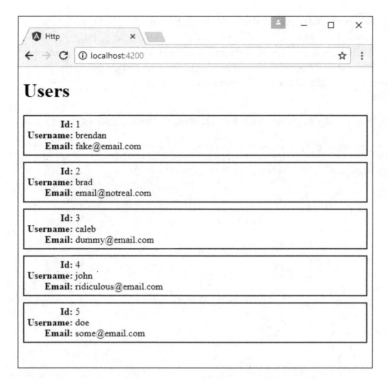

Figure 10.1   Implementing the http service to allow Angular components to interact with a web server.

Implementing a Simple Mock Server Using the http Service

The code in Listings 10.6 through 10.11 implements a simple mock web server and the Angular application that accesses it. Figure 10.2 shows the output. The web server returns a simple JSON object with a list of users. The web application uses HTTP GET, create, and delete requests to allow the user to view, add to, and remove from the list of users.

> **Note**
>
> To create the mock service, you need to run the following command from the console:
>
>   npm install Angular-in-memory-web-api
>
> This service is intended for development purposes only and shouldn't ever be used in a production application.

Listing 10.6 is the mock data service that returns the JSON object. This file will be accessed using HTTP requests, which will allow `http` to modify the database. Line 1 imports `InMemoryDbService`, which allows Angular to use this as a database where data can be stored while the session is active. The database is created and made useable on line 3, using the `createDb()` method, which returns the users as a JSON object.

Listing 10.6 `data.service.ts`: **An Angular Mock Service that Returns a JSON Object Called Users**

```
01 import { InMemoryDbService } from 'angular-in-memory-web-api';
02 export class InMemoryDataService implements InMemoryDbService {
03   createDb() {
04     const users = [
05       {
06         "id": 1,
07         "userName": "brendan",
08         "email": "fake@email.com"
09       },
10       {
11         "id": 2,
12         "userName": "brad",
13         "email": "email@notreal.com"
14       },
15       {
16         "id": 3,
17         "userName": "caleb",
18         "email": "dummy@email.com"
19       }
20     ]
21     return {users};
22   }
23 }
```

Listing 10.7 implements the Angular component. `UserService`, which is imported on line 7, contains all the HTTP functions that this application will be using. `UserService` is added to the component providers on line 13, making it available to the component. On line 19, `UserService` is implemented as a variable in the constructor.

Lines 21 through 37 defines the `deleteUser()` function, which takes in a user object. On lines 32 and 33, the `deleteUser()` function on the `UserService` is called and passes in the user ID to let the database know which user to delete. The function has a callback in the `.then()` method that calls `this.getUsers()` to refresh the current list of users.

Lines 39 through 52 define the `createUser()` function. This function takes two parameters, `username` and `email`. It assigns those parameters to a `user` object on lines 41 through 44. Lines 48 through 51 call the `createUser()` method on the `UserService` and pass in the `user` object. Once the response is received, the `createUser()` method pushes the response into the `users` array, which is reflected immediately in the DOM.

Listing 10.7 `createDelete.component.ts`: **An Angular Component that Gets and Modifies a List of Users with the `http` Service**

```
01 import { Component, OnInit } from '@angular/core';
02 import { Observable }        from 'rxjs/Observable';
03 import { Http }        from '@angular/http';
04
05 import 'rxjs/Rx';
06
07 import { UserService } from './user.service';
08
09 @Component({
10   selector: 'app-root',
11   templateUrl: './app.component.html',
12   styleUrls: ['./app.component.CSS'],
13   providers: [UserService]
14 })
15 export class AppComponent implements OnInit {
16   users = [];
17   selectedUser;
18
19   constructor(private UserService: UserService){ }
20
21   ngOnInit(){
22     this.getUsers()
23   }
24
25   getUsers(): void {
26     this.UserService
27        .getUsers()
28        .then(users => this.users = users)
29   }
30
31   deleteUser(user){
32     this.UserService
33       .deleteUser(user.id)
34       .then(() => {
35         this.getUsers();
36       });
37   }
38
39   createUser(userName, email){
40     this.selectedUser = null;
41     let user = {
42       'userName': userName.trim(),
43       'email': email.trim()
44     };
45     if (!user.userName || !user.email){
```

```
46        return;
47      }
48      this.UserService.createUser(user)
49          .then(res => {
50            this.users.push(res);
51          })
52    }
53  }
```

Listing 10.8 implements the Angular service `UserService`, which handles all theHTTP requests for the application. Lines 16 through 21 define the `deleteUser()` method, which takes in the parameter `id`. An HTTP `delete` request is then created using `id` to go to the server and delete the user with the matching ID. Lines 22 through 31 define the `createUser()` method, which takes in a user object. A `post` request passes the user to the server as a JSON string, which is then added to the server.

Listing 10.8   `user.service.ts`: **An Angular Service that Uses** `http` **to Send and Get Data from a Server**

```
01 import { Injectable } from '@angular/core';
02 import { Http }        from '@angular/http';
03 import 'rxjs/add/operator/toPromise';
04
05 @Injectable()
06 export class UserService {
07   url = 'api/users'
08   constructor(private http: Http) { }
09
10   getUsers(): Promise<any[]> {
11     return this.http.get(this.url)
12                .toPromise()
13                .then(response => response.JSON().data)
14                .catch(this.handleError)
15   }
16   deleteUser(id: number): Promise<void>{
17     return this.http.delete(`${this.url}/${id}`)
18                  .toPromise()
19                  .then(() => null)
20                  .catch(this.handleError);
21   }
22   createUser(user): Promise<any>{
23     return this.http
24              .post(this.url, JSON.stringify({
25                userName: user.userName,
26                email: user.email
27              }))
28              .toPromise()
```

```
29                .then(res => res.JSON().data)
30                .catch(this.handleError)
31    }
32
33    private handleError(error: any): Promise<any> {
34      console.error('An error occurred', error);
35      return Promise.reject(error.message || error);
36    }
37
38 }
```

Listing 10.9 implements an Angular template that utilizes ngFor to create a list of users to be displayed within the application.

Listing 10.9 createDelete.component.html: **An Angular Template that Displays a List of Users Received from the Database with Options to Create and Delete Users**

```
01 <div>
02    <label>user name:</label> <input #userName />
03    <label>user email:</label> <input #userEmail />
04    <button (click)="createUser(userName.value, userEmail.value);
05            userName.value=''; userEmail.value=''">
06      Add
07    </button>
08 </div>
09
10 <h1>
11    Users
12 </h1>
13 <div class="userCard" *ngFor="let user of users">
14    <div><span>Id:</span> {{user.id}}</div>
15    <div><span>Username:</span> {{user.userName}}</div>
16    <div><span>Email:</span> {{user.email}}</div>
17    <button class="delete"
18        (click)="deleteUser(user); $event.stopPropagation()">x</button>
19 </div>
```

Listing 10.10 is a CSS file that styles the application so that each user is distinguishable from the rest and easy to see.

Listing 10.10 createDelete.component.CSS: **A CSS Stylesheet that Styles the Application**

```
01 span{
02    width: 75px;
03    text-align: right;
04    font-weight: bold;
```

```
05    display: inline-block;
06 }
07 .userCard{
08    border: 2px ridge blue;
09    margin: 10px 0px;
10    padding: 5px;
11 }
12 .selected{
13    background-color: steelblue;
14    color: white;
15 }
```

Listing 10.11 implements an Angular module that imports the mock data service.
Line 5 imports InMemoryWebApiModule from angular-in-memory-web-api, which helps
wire the mock database into the application. Line 8 imports InMemoryDataService from
Listing 10.6. Line 18 shows InMemoryWebApiModule using its forRoot method on the
InMemoryDataService, fully making the database service available to be used by the HTTP
requests.

Listing 10.11 app.module.ts: **An Angular Module that Imports** InMemoryWebApiModule **to Be Used with the Application**

```
01 import { BrowserModule } from '@angular/platform-browser';
02 import { NgModule } from '@angular/core';
03 import { FormsModule } from '@angular/forms';
04 import { HttpModule } from '@angular/http';
05 import { InMemoryWebApiModule } from 'angular-in-memory-web-api';
06
07 import { AppComponent } from './app.component';
08 import { InMemoryDataService } from './data.service'
09
10 @NgModule({
11    declarations: [
12      AppComponent
13    ],
14    imports: [
15      BrowserModule,
16      FormsModule,
17      HttpModule,
18      InMemoryWebApiModule.forRoot(InMemoryDataService)
19    ],
20    providers: [],
21    bootstrap: [AppComponent]
22 })
23 export class AppModule { }
```

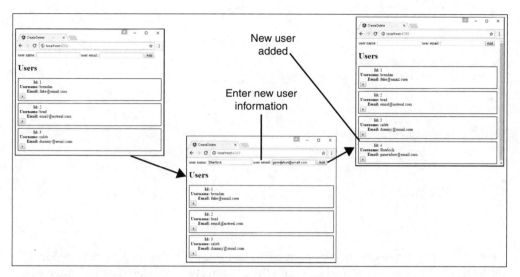

Figure 10.2   Implementing a simple mock server to create and delete items from a database

Implementing a Simple Mock Server and Using the `http` Service to Update Items on the Server

The code in Listings 10.12 through 10.16 implements the same mock web server from the previous example as well as the Angular application that accesses it. Figure 10.3 shows the output. The web application allows a user to view and edit the list of users, using HTTP `get` and `put` requests.

Listing 10.12 is the mock data service that returns the JSON object. This file will be accessed using HTTP requests, which will allow `http` to modify the database. Line 1 imports `InMemoryDbService`, which allows Angular to use this as a database where data can be stored while the session is active. The database is created and made usable on line 3, using the `createDb()` method, which returns the users as a JSON object.

Listing 10.12   `data.service.ts`: **An Angular Mock Service that Returns a JSON Object Called Users**

```
01 import { InMemoryDbService } from 'angular-in-memory-web-api';
02 export class InMemoryDataService implements InMemoryDbService {
03   createDb() {
04     const users = [
05       {
06         "id": 1,
07         "userName": "brendan",
08         "email": "fake@email.com"
```

```
09        },
10        {
11          "id": 2,
12          "userName": "brad",
13          "email": "email@notreal.com"
14        },
15        {
16          "id": 3,
17          "userName": "caleb",
18          "email": "dummy@email.com"
19        }
20      ]
21      return {users};
22    }
23  }
```

Listing 10.13 implements an Angular component that gets a list of users to be displayed in the template. This component also allows for the updating of users. Lines 7 and 13 import UserService and provide it to the component. In line 19, UserService is turned into a usable variable also named UserService. Lines 21 through 23 show the ngOnInit method, which calls the getUsers method when the component finishes loading. Lines 25 through 29 show the getUsers method, which calls the getUsers method on UserService and assigns the result to the variable users. Lines 31 through 33 show the selectUser method, which takes a parameter named user. This method assigns user to the variable selectedUser. Lines 35 through 39 show the updateUser method, which takes a parameter named user. The updateUser method sets the variable selectedUser to null and then invokes the updateUser method on userService, passing in user as a parameter. When the updateUser method completes, the getUsers method is called to refresh the list of users that is displayed.

Listing 10.13   update.component.ts: **An Angular Component that Uses** http **to Update Data in the Server**

```
01 import { Component, OnInit } from '@angular/core';
02 import { Observable }        from 'rxjs/Observable';
03 import { Http }       from '@angular/http';
04
05 import 'rxjs/Rx';
06
07 import { UserService } from './user.service';
08
09 @Component({
10   selector: 'app-root',
11   templateUrl: './app.component.html',
12   styleUrls: ['./app.component.CSS'],
13   providers: [UserService]
14 })
```

```
15 export class AppComponent implements OnInit {
16   users = [];
17   selectedUser;
18
19   constructor(private UserService: UserService){ }
20
21   ngOnInit(){
22     this.getUsers()
23   }
24
25   getUsers(): void {
26     this.UserService
27       .getUsers()
28       .then(users => this.users = users)
29   }
30
31   selectUser(user){
32     this.selectedUser = user;
33   }
34
35   updateUser(user){
36     this.selectedUser = null;
37     this.UserService.updateUser(user)
38     .then(() => this.getUsers());
39   }
40 }
```

Listing 10.14 implements the Angular service `UserService`, which handles all the HTTP
requests for the application. Lines 16 through 24 define the `updateUser` method, which takes
in the parameter `user`. A URL is then generated to specify which user will be updated. An
HTTP `put` request is made on line 20, taking in the generated URL and the `user` object, which
is passed into the `json.stringify` method. the `updateUser` method then sends a `response`
object on success or moves to the error handler on fail.

Listing 10.14 `user.service.ts`: **An Angular Service that Gets Users and Updates a User**

```
01 import { Injectable } from '@angular/core';
02 import { Http }       from '@angular/http';
03 import 'rxjs/add/operator/toPromise';
04
05 @Injectable()
06 export class UserService {
07   url = 'api/users'
08   constructor(private http: Http) { }
09
```

```
10   getUsers(): Promise<any[]> {
11     return this.http.get(this.url)
12               .toPromise()
13               .then(response => response.JSON().data)
14               .catch(this.handleError)
15   }
16   updateUser(user): Promise<void>{
17     console.log(user);
18     const url = `${this.url}/${user.id}`;
19     return this.http
20       .put(url, JSON.stringify(user))
21       .toPromise()
22       .then(() => user)
23       .catch(this.handleError)
24   }
25
26   private handleError(error: any): Promise<any> {
27     console.error('An error occurred', error);
28     return Promise.reject(error.message || error);
29   }
30
31 }
```

Listing 10.15 implements an Angular template that uses `ngFor` to create a list of users to be displayed within the application. These users are each selectable. When one is selected, the information is shown in an editable form field that allows the user to be edited and saved. Lines 20 through 24 show the button that can be clicked to invoke the `updateUser` method and pass in an object with that user's updated information.

Listing 10.15 `update.component.html`: **An Angular Template that Displays a List of Users and Can Be Updated**

```
01 <h1>
02   Users
03 </h1>
04 <div class="userCard" *ngFor="let user of users"
05     (click)="selectUser(user)"
06     [class.selected]="user === selectedUser">
07   <div><span>Id:</span> {{user.id}}</div>
08   <div><span>Username:</span> {{user.userName}}</div>
09   <div><span>Email:</span> {{user.email}}</div>
10 </div>
11
```

```
12 <div *ngIf="selectedUser">
13   <label>user name:</label>
14   <input #updateName [ngModel]="selectedUser.userName"/>
15
16   <label>user email:</label>
17   <input #updateEmail [ngModel]="selectedUser.email" />
18
19
20   <button (click)="updateUser(
21       {'id': selectedUser.id,
22        'userName': updateName.value,
23        'email': updateEmail.value});
24   ">
25     Save
26   </button>
27 </div>
```

Listing 10.16 is a CSS file that styles the application so that each user is distinguishable from the rest and easy to see. It provides some logic to help the user know that each user can be clicked on.

Listing 10.16   update.component.CSS: **A CSS File that Styles the Application**

```
01 span{
02   width: 75px;
03   text-align: right;
04   font-weight: bold;
05   display: inline-block;
06 }
07 .userCard{
08   border: 2px ridge blue;
09   margin: 10px 0px;
10   padding: 5px;
11   cursor: pointer;
12 }
13 .userCard:hover{
14   background-color: lightblue;
15 }
16 .selected{
17   background-color: steelblue;
18   color: white;
19 }
```

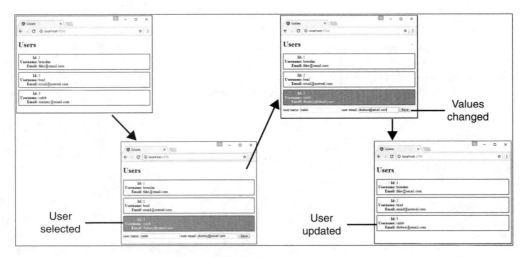

Figure 10.3   Implementing a simple mock server to update items in a database

Changing Views with the `router` Service

The `router` service enables you to change views on the web application so that you can route back and forth between components. This can be done as a full-page view change or can change smaller segments of a single-page application. The `router` service is in an external angular module called `RouterModule` and needs to be included in the applications module to be used throughout the application.

To set up an app for routing, you need to import the `Routes` and `Router` modules from @ angular/router. To help keep the application simple to maintain, `router` should get its own module that can be imported into the main application module.

Defining routes for an application is as simple as making an array of objects, with each object defining a specific route. The two required options for each of these routes are `path` and `component`. The `path` option specifies the tree to follow to reach the component. The `component` option defines which component will be loaded into the view. The following examples show the syntax for defining a `Routes` array:

```
Const routes: Routes = [
  {
    Path: '',
    Component: myComponent
  },
  {
    Path: 'route',
    Component: myComponent
  },
```

```
{
  Path: 'routeWithParams/:param1/:param2',
  Component: myComponent
}
]
```

Many more parameters can be added to the `route` object. Table 10.3 shows a list of some of them.

Table 10.3 **Properties that Can Be Defined in the `config` Parameter for `route` Service Object**

Property	Description
`path`	Shows where in the router tree this route belongs
`component`	Defines which component will be loaded once routed
`redirectTo`	Redirects to the defined path instead of the current route
`outlet`	Specifies the name used for the `RouterOutlet` that renders the route
`canActivate`	Protects the route by preventing activation when `false`
`canActivateChild`	Protects the child routes by preventing activation when `false`
`canDeactivate`	Specifies whether the route can be deactivated
`canLoad`	Allows you to protect specific modules from being loaded in the route
`Data`	Allows for data to be passed into the component
`Resolve`	Specifies a resolver that pre-fetches data for the route before activation
`Children`	Allows for a nested routes array that contains route objects (Each of these objects has the same options described in this table.)
`loadChildren`	Allows for lazy loading of child routes
`runGaurdsAndResolvers`	Defines when the guards and resolvers are run

Once the `routes` array is defined, it needs to be implemented into the router so that the `router` service knows it exists and knows how to use it. This is done by using the `forRoot` method on `RouterModule`. The result of this is included in the `routing` module's `imports` array. The syntax for this looks as follows:

```
imports: [RouterModule.forRoot(routes)]
```

Using `routes` in Angular

To use `routes` in Angular, the `routing` module needs to be included within the main app module and included within the imports—the same as for built-in Angular modules. Once it is included within the application module, the defined routes become available throughout the application.

To be able to use `router` within a component, `Router` and `ActivatedRoute` need to be imported from `@angular/router`. Once they are imported, they need to be implemented via the constructor. The following code shows the syntax:

```
Constructor(
    private route: ActivatedRoute,
    private router: Router
){}
```

There are two ways to navigate between routes. The first way is from HTML directly, using the Angular directive `routerLink`, which has the following syntax:

```
<a routerLink="/myRoute">
```

The second way to navigate between routes is from the component class, using the following syntax:

```
myFunction(){
    this.router.navigate(['myRoute'])
}
```

When the router is all wired up and ready to be used, the last step is to make sure the routes get displayed on the application. You do this by using the Angular HTML tag `router-outlet`. It is important to note that the component that uses `router-outlet` will be outside the router, and anything besides `router-outlet` will always display, no matter what route is currently being shown. You can implement `router-outlet` by using the following syntax:

```
<router-outlet></router-outlet>
```

Implementing a Simple Router

Listings 10.17 through 10.23 implement a simple router that allows the user to navigate between two components. Figure 10.4 shows the output. This router is navigated using the Angular `routerLink` directive within the HTML, allowing it to change between the views.

Listing 10.17 shows the application module, which is the main module for the application. `App.module` imports the `Router` module from Listing 10.17. On line 6, this file loads `AppRoutingModule`, which is added to the `imports` array on line 21.

Listing 10.17 `app.module.ts`: **An Angular Module that Imports the** `Router` **Module File**

```
01 import { BrowserModule } from '@angular/platform-browser';
02 import { NgModule } from '@angular/core';
03 import { FormsModule } from '@angular/forms';
04 import { HttpModule } from '@angular/http';
05
```

```
06 import { AppRoutingModule } from './app-routing.module';
07 import { AppComponent } from './app.component';
08 import { Route2Component } from './route2/route2.component';
09 import { HomeComponent } from './home/home.component';
10
11 @NgModule({
12   declarations: [
13     AppComponent,
14     Route2Component,
15     HomeComponent
16   ],
17   imports: [
18     BrowserModule,
19     FormsModule,
20     HttpModule,
21     AppRoutingModule
22   ],
23   providers: [],
24   bootstrap: [AppComponent]
25 })
26 export class AppModule { }
```

Listing 10.18 shows the `Router` module, which defines the routes for the application. The `Router` module imports `Routes` and `RouterModule` to enable routing within the application. The `Router` module also imports any components that will be used as routes. Lines 5 through 14 define the `routes` array, which contains the route definitions for the application. Lines 6 through 9 define the home route that the application will default to because the path is set to an empty string. The home route uses `HomeComponent` as the component that controls the view. Lines 10 through 13 define a second route object that will be displayed when the path is set to `route2`. This route uses `Route2Component`.

Listing 10.18 `app-routing.module.ts`: **An Angular Module that Defines the** `routes` **for This Application**

```
01 import { NgModule } from '@angular/core';
02 import { Routes, RouterModule } from '@angular/router';
03 import { Route2Component } from './route2/route2.component';
04 import { HomeComponent } from './home/home.component';
05 const routes: Routes = [
06   {
07     path: '',
08     component: HomeComponent
09   },
10   {
11     path: 'route2',
12     component: Route2Component
13   }
```

```
14 ];
15
16 @NgModule({
17   imports: [RouterModule.forRoot(routes)],
18   exports: [RouterModule]
19 })
20 export class AppRoutingModule { }
```

Listing 10.19 shows the root component for the application. This component has a simple template that outputs `router-outlet` for `router` to display its routes.

Listing 10.19 `app.component.ts`: **An Angular Component that Defines the Router Outlet**

```
01 import { Component } from '@angular/core';
02
03 @Component({
04   selector: 'app-root',
05   template: '<router-outlet></router-outlet>'
06 })
07 export class AppComponent {}
```

Listing 10.20 shows the home component template file. This file displays a message that lets the user know that the route is working, followed by a link that uses `routerLink` to navigate the user to a separate view.

Listing 10.20 `home.component.html`: **An HTML File that Is the Default Displayed Route**

```
01 <p>
02   Home Route works!
03 </p>
04 <a routerLink="/route2">Route 2</a>
```

Listing 10.21 shows the home component file. This file is as barebones as a component gets. Its main purpose is to load the template file and make it available to the router.

Listing 10.21 `home.component.ts`: **An Angular Component that Includes a Template with a Route**

```
01 import { Component} from '@angular/core';
02
03 @Component({
04   selector: 'app-home',
05   templateUrl: './home.component.html',
06   styleUrls: ['./home.component.CSS']
07 })
08 export class HomeComponent{}
```

Listing 10.22 shows the `route2` component template file. This file displays a message that lets the user know the route is working, followed by a link that uses `routerLink` to navigate the user to a separate view.

Listing 10.22   `route2.component.html`: **A CSS File that Styles the Application**

```
01 <p>
02    route 2 works!
03 </p>
04 <a routerLink="/">Route 1</a>
```

Listing 10.23 shows the barebones `route2` component file. Its main purpose is to load the template file and make it available to the router.

Listing 10.23   `route2.component.ts`: **An Angular Component that Includes a Template with a Route**

```
01 import { Component } from '@angular/core';
02
03 @Component({
04    selector: 'app-route2',
05    templateUrl: './route2.component.html'
06 })
07 export class Route2Component {}
```

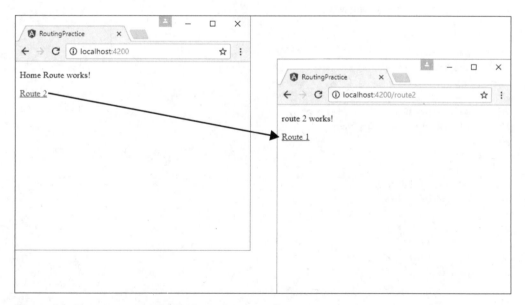

Figure 10.4   Implementing the `http` service to allow Angular components to interact with a web server

Implementing a Router with a Navigation Bar

The code in Listings 10.24 through 10.35 implements a router with a nav bar that allows the user to navigate between views that are nested. Figure 10.5 shows the output. This router is navigated using the Angular `routerLink` directive within the HTML, allowing it to change between the views.

Listing 10.24 shows the `Router` module, which defines the routes for the application. The `Router` module imports any components that will be used as routes. There isn't a home route for this example. If the route is empty, the router redirects to `page1`, as shown in lines 22 through 25. In addition, if an invalid route is typed into the URL, the router again redirects to `page1`, as shown in lines 27 through 30.

Listing 10.24 `app-routing.module.ts`: **An Angular Module that Defines the Routes for the Application**

```
01 import { NgModule } from '@angular/core';
02 import { Routes, RouterModule } from '@angular/router';
03 import { Page1Component } from './page1/page1.component';
04 import { Page2Component } from './page2/page2.component';
05 import { Page3Component } from './page3/page3.component';
06 import { Page4Component } from './page4/page4.component';
07 import { NavComponent } from './nav/nav.component';
08 const routes: Routes = [
09   {
10     path: 'page1',
11     component: Page1Component
12   },
13   {
14     path: 'page2',
15     component: Page2Component
16   },
17   {
18     path: 'page3',
19     component: Page3Component
20   },
21   {
22     path: '',
23     redirectTo: '/page1',
24     pathMatch: 'full'
25   },
26   {
27     path: '**',
28     redirectTo: '/page1',
29     pathMatch: 'full'
30   }
31 ];
32
```

```
33 @NgModule({
34   imports: [RouterModule.forRoot(routes)],
35   exports: [RouterModule]
36 })
37 export class AppRoutingModule { }
```

Listing 10.25 shows the nav component, which controls the nav bar and links to the views within the page. Lines 9 through 19 show an array of available pages which the nav bar can use to create buttons with links for navigation.

Listing 10.25 `nav.component.ts`: **An Angular Component that Creates a Persisting Nav Bar That Navigates Between Views**

```
01 import { Component, OnInit } from '@angular/core';
02
03 @Component({
04   selector: 'app-nav',
05   templateUrl: './nav.component.html',
06   styleUrls: ['./nav.component.CSS']
07 })
08 export class NavComponent{
09   pages = [
10     { 'url': 'page1',
11       'text': 'page 1'
12     },
13     { 'url': 'page2',
14       'text': 'page 2'
15     },
16     { 'url': 'page3',
17       'text': 'page 3'
18     }
19   ]
20 }
```

Listing 10.26 shows the nav component template file. It creates a list of buttons that allow for navigation between the named routes.

Listing 10.26 `nav.component.html`: **An Angular Template that Creates the View for the Nav Bar**

```
01 <span class="container" *ngFor="let page of pages">
02   <a routerLink="/{{page.url}}">{{page.text}}</a>
03 </span>
```

Listing 10.27 shows the nav component CSS file. This file styles the nav bar buttons so they make sense. Lines 9 through 12 cause the color of the buttons and text to change when the user hovers the mouse over a button.

Listing 10.27 `nav.component.CSS`: **A CSS File that Styles the Navigation Buttons for the Application**

```
01 a{
02   padding: 5px 10px;
03   border: 1px solid darkblue;
04   background-color: steelblue;
05   color: white;
06   text-decoration: none;
07   border-radius: 3px;
08 }
09 a:hover{
10   color: black;
11   background-color: lightgrey;
12 }
```

Listing 10.28 shows the root component file `app.component.ts`, which serves as the entry to the application and loads the routed views and the nav component.

Listing 10.28 `app.comonent.ts`: **An Angular Component that Acts as the Root Component for the Application**

```
01 import { Component } from '@angular/core';
02
03 @Component({
04   selector: 'app-root',
05   templateUrl: './app.component.html',
06   styleUrls: ['./app.component.CSS']
07 })
08 export class AppComponent { }
```

Listing 10.29 shows the root component template file, which loads the nav component followed by the router outlet, which is where the views are loaded for the application.

Listing 10.29 `app.component.html`: **An Angular Template that Loads the Nav Component Followed by the Router Outlet**

```
01 <div><app-nav></app-nav></div>
02 <div><router-outlet></router-outlet></div>
```

Listing 10.30 shows the root component CSS file, which provides some spacing for the nav bar so it is displayed nicely.

Listing 10.30 `app.component.CSS`: **An Angular Module that Imports the** `Router` **Module File**

```
01 div{
02   margin: 15px 0px;
03 }
```

Listing 10.31 shows the page1 component. This component loads a template that will be used as one of the views for this application. Line 5 loads an image to be displayed on the view.

Listing 10.31 `page1.component.ts`: **An Angular Module that Imports the** `Router` **Module File**

```
01 import { Component } from '@angular/core';
02
03 @Component({
04   selector: 'app-page1',
05   template: '<img src="../assets/images/lake.jpg" />'
06 })
07 export class Page1Component {}
```

Listing 10.32 shows the page2 component. This component loads a template that will be used as one of the views for this application.

Listing 10.32 `page2.component.ts`: **An Angular Module that Imports the** `Router` **Module File**

```
01 import { Component } from '@angular/core';
02
03 @Component({
04   selector: 'app-page2',
05   templateUrl: './page2.component.html'
06 })
07 export class Page2Component { }
```

Listing 10.33 shows the page2 template file, which contains some dummy text that will be loaded into the view.

Listing 10.33 `page2.component.html`: **An Angular Template that Creates the View for Page 2**

```
01 <p>
02   Lorem ipsum dolor sit amet, consectetur adipiscing elit. Nam efficitur
03   tristique ornare. Interdum et malesuada fames ac ante ipsum primis in
04   faucibus. Proin id nulla vitae arcu laoreet consequat. Donec quis
05   convallis felis. Mauris ultricies consectetur lectus, a hendrerit leo
06   feugiat sit amet. Aliquam nec velit nibh. Nam interdum turpis ac dui
07   congue maximus. Integer fringilla ante vitae arcu molestie finibus. Morbi
08   eget ex pellentesque, convallis orci venenatis, vehicula nunc.
09 </p>
```

Listing 10.34 shows the `page3` component. This component loads a template that will be used as one of the views for this application.

Listing 10.34 `page3.component.ts`: **An Angular Module that Imports the** `Router` **Module File**

```
01 import { Component } from '@angular/core';
02
03 @Component({
04   selector: 'app-page3',
05   templateUrl: './page3.component.html'
06 })
07 export class Page3Component {}
```

Listing 10.35 shows the `page3` template file, which creates a text area box to be displayed on the view.

Listing 10.35 `page3.component.html`: **An Angular Template that Creates the View for Page 3**

```
01 <textarea rows="4" cols="50" placeHolder="Some Text Here">
02 </textarea>
```

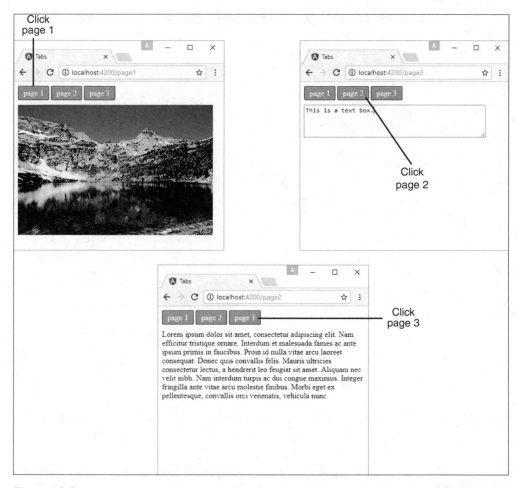

Figure 10.5   Implementing the `http` service to allow Angular components to interact with a web server

Implementing a Router with Parameters

Listings 10.36 through 10.40 implement a router with a route that takes in a parameter that allows for data to be transferred to that view through the `url` parameter. Figure 10.6 shows the output.

Listing 10.36 shows the `Router` module, which defines the routes for the application. The `Router` module imports any components that will be used as routes. Line 14 defines the path to page 2, which takes in the parameter `this.text`.

Listing 10.36 `app-routing.module.ts`: **An Angular Template that Assigns Router Parameters**

```
01 import { Component } from '@angular/core';
02 import { Router, ActivatedRoute, Params } from '@angular/router';
03
04 @Component({
05   selector: 'app-page1',
06   templateUrl: './page1.component.html'
07 })
08 export class Page1Component {
09   text='';
10   constructor(
11     private route: ActivatedRoute,
12     private router: Router,
13   ){ }
14   gotoPage2(){
15     this.router.navigate(
16         ['/page2', this.text],
17         {
18           relativeTo: this.route,
19           skipLocationChange: true
20         }
21     );
22   }
23 }
```

Listing 10.37 shows the root component `app.component.ts`. This file has a template that declares `router-outlet` to display the views from the router.

Listing 10.37 `app.component.ts`: **An Angular Component that Acts as the Entry Point to the Application**

```
01 import { Component } from '@angular/core';
02
03 @Component({
04   selector: 'app-root',
05   template: '<router-outlet></router-outlet>'
06 })
07 export class AppComponent { }
```

Listing 10.38 shows the `page1` component. This component imports `Router` and `ActivatedRoute` from `@angular/router` to allow this component to access the router and read or assign parameters to `RouterState`. Lines 10 through 13 define the constructor, which on lines 11 and 12 implements `ActivatedRoute` and `Router` as private variables `route` and `router`. Lines 14 through 22 define the function `gotoPage2()`, which navigates to `page2`, passing in a parameter. Line 16 navigates to `page2`, passing in `this.text` as the parameter. Lines 18 and 19 allow the application to change views without changing the URL in the browser.

Listing 10.38 `page1.component.ts`: **An Angular Component that Navigates to Page 2 with Parameters**

```
01 import { Component } from '@angular/core';
02 import { Router, ActivatedRoute } from '@angular/router';
03
04 @Component({
05   selector: 'app-page1',
06   templateUrl: './page1.component.html'
07 })
08 export class Page1Component {
09   text='';
10   constructor(
11     private route: ActivatedRoute,
12     private router: Router,
13   ){ }
14   gotoPage2(){
15     this.router.navigate(
16         ['/page2', this.text],
17         {
18           relativeTo: this.route,
19           skipLocationChange: true
20         }
21     );
22   }
23 }
```

Listing 10.39 shows the `page1` template file. Line 4 shows a text area that is bound to the variable text that is passed as a parameter when routed to page 2. Line 5 creates a button that invokes the `gotoPage2` function, changing the view. This button is available only when the variable text has a non-empty value.

Listing 10.39 `page1.component.html`: **An HTML Template that Provides an Input Field to Give a Value to Router Parameters**

```
01 <span>
02   Enter Text to Pass As Params:
03 </span>
04 <input type=text [(ngModel)]="text" />
05 <button [disabled]="!text" (click)="gotoPage2()">Page 2</button>
```

Listing 10.40 shows the `page2` component. This component imports `Router` and `ActivatedRoute` from `@angular/router` to allow this component to access the router and parameters that were set when the route was loaded. Lines 15 and 16 create a subscription to the `params` observable and assign the value to the variable `text` to be displayed in the view.

Listing 10.40   `page2.component.ts`: **An Angular Component that Displays Router Parameters on the View**

```
01 import { Component, OnInit } from '@angular/core';
02 import { Router, ActivatedRoute } from '@angular/router';
03
04 @Component({
05   selector: 'app-page2',
06   templateUrl: './page2.component.html'
07 })
08 export class Page2Component implements OnInit {
09   text;
10   constructor(
11     private route: ActivatedRoute,
12     private router: Router
13   ) { }
14   ngOnInit() {
15     this.route.params
16         .subscribe(text => this.text = text.params);
17   }
18
19   goBack(){
20     this.router.navigate(['/page1']);
21   }
22 }
```

Listing 10.41 shows the `page2`template file. Line 2 displays the variable `text`, which gets its value from the route `params`. Line 3 creates a button that can be clicked to navigate back to page 1.

Listing 10.41   `page2.component.html`: **Parameters Passed from the Router**

```
01 <h3>Params From Page 1</h3>
02 <p>{{text}}</p>
03 <button (click)="goBack()" >back</button>
```

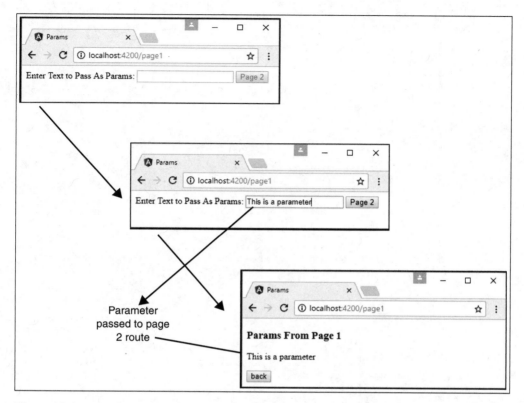

Figure 10.6   Implementing the `http` service to allow Angular components to interact with a web server.

Summary

Angular services are objects that contain functionality you can inject into other Angular components. Angular's built-in services provide a lot of prebuilt functionality needed for your client code. For example, the `http` service allows you to easily integrate web server communication into your Angular applications, and the `router` service allows you to manage navigation between views.

Creating Your Own Custom Angular Services

Angular provides a lot of functionality in its built-in services, but it also allows you to implement your own custom services to provide specific functionality. You should implement a custom service any time you need to provide task-based functionality to an application.

When implementing custom services, you need to think about each service as being a chunk of reusable code that performs one or more related tasks. Then you can design and group them together into libraries that can easily be consumed by several different Angular applications.

This chapter introduces Angular custom services. It provides several examples of custom Angular services to provide you with a clearer understanding of how to design and build your own.

Integrating Custom Services into Angular Applications

As you begin implementing Angular services for your applications, you will find that some will be very simple and others will be very complex. The complexity of the service typically reflects the complexity of the underlying data and the functionality it provides. The purpose of this section is to provide you with some basic examples of different types of custom services to illustrate how they can be implemented and used. Table 11.1 lists some uses for services.

Table 11.1   **Use Cases for Custom Services**

Service	Description
Mock service	Provides dummy data that can be used to test HTTP-based services while the back end is unavailable
Constant data	Returns data variables that need to remain constant, such as the mathematical value of pi
Variable data	Returns data variables that can be changed, with the changed value being saved to the service for other services to use

Service	Description
HTTP connection to the back end	Should be used within a custom service to create an interface with the back-end data
Data transformations	Takes in a form of data to be transformed, runs the transformation, and returns the transformed value (for example, a square service that takes in a number and returns the square)
Shared service	Any type of service that can be used by multiple components at once while the data is automatically updated for all components any time it changes

Adding an Angular Service to an Application

This section goes over how to create and implement a custom service in an application. When you create services, they have to be made injectable in order to be used throughout the application. The following example shows the syntax for creating an injectable service:

```
import { Injectable } from '@angular/core';
@Injectable()
export class CustomService { }
```

Once you've created an injectable service, it needs to be imported and provided to any Angular component that needs access to it. The following is the syntax for importing a custom service, as along with the custom service being injected via the `providers` array in the component decorator metadata:

```
import { CustomService } from './path_to_service';

@Component({
  selector: 'app-root',
  template: '',
  providers: [ CustomService ]
})
```

The final step in making a custom service usable is to create an instance of that service to be used throughout the component. You do this in the constructor of the component, as shown in the following example:

```
constructor(
  private myService: CustomService
){}
```

When these steps are complete, the custom service and any of its methods are made available to the component through the instance `myService`.

The following sections provide examples that illustrate various ways of implementing custom services.

Implementing a Simple Application that Uses a Constant Data Service

This example shows how to build a constant data service. The purpose of this example is to create a simple service that returns a constant data variable.

Listing 11.1 shows the `pi` service, which returns the value of pi. Lines 1 and 3 import and implement `Injectable` to make the service available to be used externally. Line 4 creates the `PiService` class, which holds the definition for the service. Lines 5 through 7 define the `getPi` method, which returns the value of pi.

Listing 11.1   `pi.service.ts`: **Creating a Service that Returns the Value of Pi**

```
01 import { Injectable } from '@angular/core';
02
03 @Injectable()
04 export class PiService {
05   getPi(){
06     return Math.PI;
07   }
08 }
```

Listing 11.2 implements an Angular component that imports and implements `PiService`. Lines 2 and 7 show `PiService` being imported and then provided to make it available to use throughout the component. Line 12 shows `PiService` being instantiated as the variable `PiService`. Lines 14 through 16 show the `ngOnInit` method, which calls the `getPi` method from `PiService` and assigns it to the variable `pi`.

Listing 11.2   `app.component.ts`: **An Angular Component that Gets the Value of Pi from PiService**

```
01 import { Component, OnInit } from '@angular/core';
02 import { PiService } from './pi.service';
03
04 @Component({
05   selector: 'app-root',
06   templateUrl: './app.component.html',
07   providers: [ PiService ]
08 })
09 export class AppComponent implements OnInit {
10   pi: number;
11   constructor(
12     private PiService: PiService
13   ){}
14   ngOnInit(){
15     this.pi = this.PiService.getPi();
16   }
17 }
```

Listing 11.3 shows an Angular template that displays the value of pi to five places.

Listing 11.3 `app.component.html`: **An Angular Template That Displays the Value of Pi to Five Places**

```
01 <h1>
02    Welcome. this app returns the value of pi
03 </h1>
04 <p> the value of pi is: {{pi | number:'1.1-5'}}</p>
```

Figure 11.1 shows the output of this example in a web browser.

Figure 11.1   An HTML page that shows the Angular component displaying the value of pi obtained from a constant service

Implementing a Data Transform Service

This example shows how to build a simple data transform service that takes in data variables, calculates the area of a shape, and returns the area for the shape.

Listing 11.4 shows a custom service named `AreaCalcService`, which has several methods named after various shapes. Each of these methods takes in variables that are then used to generate the areas of the shapes they are named after. Lines 1 and 3 import and implement `Injectable` to make the service available to be used externally.

Listing 11.4 `area-calc.service.ts`: **An Angular Service with Methods that Calculate the Areas of Shapes**

```
01 import { Injectable } from '@angular/core';
02
03 @Injectable()
04 export class AreaCalcService {
05    circle(radius:number): number {
06       return Math.PI * radius * radius;
07    }
```

```
08    square(base:number): number {
09      return base * base;
10    }
11    rectangle(base:number, height): number {
12      return base * height;
13    }
14    triangle(base:number, height): number {
15      return (base*height)/2;
16    }
17    trapezoid(base1:number,
18              base2:number,
19              height:number): number {
20      return ((base1+base2)/2)*height;
21    }
22 }
```

Listing 11.5 shows an Angular component that gets areas of shapes from `AreaCalcService`, based on the values received from the user. Lines 2 and 8 import `AreaCalcService` and add it to the providers to make it available to the component. Line 21 creates an instance of `AreaCalcService` as `areaCalc` to be used with the component methods.

Lines 23 through 25 define the `doCircle` method, which implements the `circle` method on `areaCalc` to get the area of a circle.

Lines 26 through 28 define the `doSquare` method, which implements the `square` method on `areaCalc` to get the area of a square.

Lines 29 through 31 define the `doRectangle` method, which implements the `rectangle` method on `areaCalc` to get the area of a rectangle.

Lines 32 through 34 define the `doTriangle` method, which implements the `triangle` method on `areaCalc` to get the area of a square.

Lines 35 through 39 define the `doTrapezoid` method, which implements the `trapezoid` method on `areaCalc` to get the area of a trapezoid.

Listing 11.5 `app.component.ts`: **An Angular Component that Gets Areas of Shapes from** `AreaCalcService` **Based on Values Received from the User**

```
01 import { Component } from '@angular/core';
02 import { AreaCalcService } from './area-calc.service';
03
04 @Component({
05   selector: 'app-root',
06   templateUrl: './app.component.html',
07   styleUrls: ['./app.component.css'],
08   providers: [ AreaCalcService ]
09 })
```

```
10 export class AppComponent {
11   circleRadius: number = 0;
12   squareBase: number = 0;
13   rectangleBase: number = 0;
14   rectangleHeight: number = 0;
15   triangleBase: number = 0;
16   triangleHeight: number = 0;
17   trapezoidBase1: number = 0;
18   trapezoidBase2: number = 0;
19   trapezoidHeight: number = 0;
20
21   constructor(private areaCalc: AreaCalcService){ }
22
23   doCircle(){
24     return this.areaCalc.circle(this.circleRadius);
25   }
26   doSquare(){
27     return this.areaCalc.square(this.squareBase);
28   }
29   doRectangle(){
30     return this.areaCalc.rectangle(this.rectangleBase, this.rectangleHeight);
31   }
32   doTriangle(){
33     return this.areaCalc.triangle(this.triangleBase, this.triangleHeight);
34   }
35   doTrapezoid(){
36     return this.areaCalc.trapezoid(this.trapezoidBase1,
37                                    this.trapezoidBase2,
38                                    this.trapezoidHeight);
39   }
40 }
```

Listing 11.6 shows an Angular template file that creates form fields to input data required to calculate the areas of various shapes. When the data is input, the area is immediately calculated and displayed to the user.

Listing 11.6 `app.component.html`: **An Angular Template that Provides a User Interface to Create Form Fields to Receive the Areas of Shapes**

```
01 <label>Circle Radius:</label>
02 <input type="text" [(ngModel)]="circleRadius"/>
03 <span>Area: {{this.doCircle()}}</span>
04 <hr>
05
06 <label>Square Side:</label>
07 <input type="text" [(ngModel)]="squareBase" />
08 <span>Area: {{this.doSquare()}}</span>
```

```
09 <hr>
10
11 <label>Rectangle Base:</label>
12 <input type="text" [(ngModel)]="rectangleBase" /> <br>
13 <label>Rectangle Height:</label>
14 <input type="text" [(ngModel)]="rectangleHeight" />
15 <span>Area: {{this.doRectangle()}}</span>
16 <hr>
17
18 <label>Triangle Base:</label>
19 <input type="text"
20   [(ngModel)]="triangleBase" /> <br>
21 <label>Triangle Height:</label>
22 <input type="text" [(ngModel)]="triangleHeight" />
23 <span>Area: {{this.doTriangle()}}</span>
24 <hr>
25
26 <label>Trapezoid Base1:</label>
27 <input type="text" [(ngModel)]="trapezoidBase1" /> <br>
28 <label>Trapezoid Base2:</label>
29 <input type="text" [(ngModel)]="trapezoidBase2" /><br>
30 <label>Trapezoid Height:</label>
31 <input type="text" [(ngModel)]="trapezoidHeight" />
32 <span>Area: {{this.doTrapezoid()}}</span>
33
```

Listing 11.7 shows a CSS file that styles the application, separating the individual forms for each shape.

Listing 11.7   `app.component.html`: **A CSS File that Styles the Application**

```
01 label{
02     color: blue;
03     font: bold 20px times new roman;
04     width:200px;
05     display: inline-block;
06     text-align: right;
07 }
08 input{
09     width:40px;
10     text-align:right;
11 }
12 span{
13     font: bold 20px courier new;
14     padding-left: 10px;
15 }
```

Figure 11.2 shows the resulting Angular application web page. As values are added to the component, the areas are automatically calculated by the custom service.

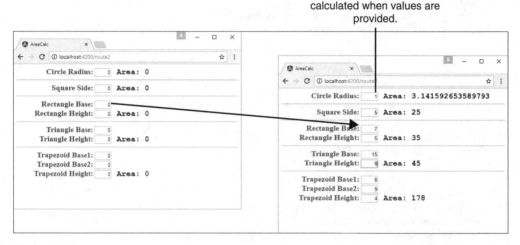

Figure 11.2   An Angular application that uses a custom service to automatically calculate the areas of different shapes

Implementing a Variable Data Service

This example shows how to build a variable data service that creates an image changer that at random times randomly selects an image from a list and sends it to the component to be displayed.

Listing 11.8 shows a custom service named RandomImageService that selects an image URL from a list and emits that URL at a random interval. Line 2 shows Observable being imported from rxjs/observable. Lines 33 through 37 show the constructor that initializes the observable imageChange and calls the method changeLoop, passing in the observer object. Lines 28 through 51 define the changeLoop method, which takes in the observable response object observer. A setTimeout function is called with a random time before it completes. Then a random image is selected from the images array. The image URL, title, and width are then emitted, and changeLoop recursively calls itself. Lines 52 through 54 define the getRandom function, which takes in two parameters, min and max, and gets a random number between those values.

Listing 11.8   `random-image.service.ts`: **An Angular Service that returns an Observable that contains a random image**

```
01 import { Injectable, OnInit } from '@angular/core';
02 import { Observable } from 'rxjs/observable';
03
04 @Injectable()
05 export class RandomImageService {
06   imageChange: Observable<any>;
07   private images = [
08     {
09       url: '../../assets/images/arch.jpg',
10       title: "Delicate Arch"
11     },
12     {
13       url: '../../assets/images/lake.jpg',
14       title: "Silver Lake"
15     },
16     {
17       url: '../../assets/images/cliff.jpg',
18       title: "Desert Cliff"
19     },
20     {
21       url: '../../assets/images/bison.jpg',
22       title: "Bison"
23     },
24     {
25       url: '../../assets/images/flower.jpg',
26       title: "Flower"
27     },
28     {
29       url: '../../assets/images/volcano.jpg',
30       title: "Volcano"
31     },
32   ];
33   constructor() {
34     this.imageChange = new Observable(observer => {
35         this.changeLoop(observer);
36       });
37   }
38   changeLoop(observer){
39     setTimeout(() => {
40       let imgIndex = this.getRandom(0,6);
41       let image = this.images[imgIndex];
42       observer.next(
43         {
44           url: image.url,
```

```
45              title: image.title,
46              width: this.getRandom(200,400)
47          }
48        );
49        this.changeLoop(observer);
50      }, this.getRandom(100,1000));
51    }
52    getRandom(min, max) {
53      return Math.floor(Math.random() * (max - min)) + min;
54    }
55    getRandomImage(): Observable<any> {
56      return this.imageChange;
57    }
58 }
```

Listing 11.9 shows an Angular component that gets a random image from
RandomImageService, displays it in the main view, and adds it into the imageHistory array.
Lines 4 and 10 show RandomImageService being imported and provided to the component. Line 17 instantiates the RandomImageService as the variable randomImages. Lines 19
through 23 create a default initial imageInfo object to hold a place until data can be received
from RandomImageService. Lines 25 through 32 show the ngOnInit method, which calls
the getRandomImage method on the randomImages service instance and assigns it to the
observable randomImage. imageInfo is then assigned the value of anything emitted from
the observable. imageHistory also adds the value of anything emitted from the observable.

Listing 11.9   app.component.ts: **An Angular Component that Gets a Random Image from**
RandomImageService **and Displays That Image**

```
01 import { Component, OnInit } from '@angular/core';
02 import { Observable } from 'rxjs/observable';
03 import { Subscription } from 'rxjs/Subscription';
04 import { RandomImageService } from './random-image.service';
05
06 @Component({
07   selector: 'app-root',
08   templateUrl: './app.component.html',
09   styleUrls: ['./app.component.css'],
10   providers: [ RandomImageService ]
11 })
12 export class AppComponent {
13   title = 'app';
14   randomImage: Observable<any>;
15   imageInfo: any;
16   imageHistory: any[];
17   constructor(
18     private randomImages: RandomImageService
```

```
19    ){
20      this.imageInfo = {
21        url: '',
22        title: 'Loading . . .',
23        width: 400
24      };
25      this.imageHistory = [];
26    }
27    ngOnInit(){
28      this.randomImage = this.randomImages.getRandomImage();
29      this.randomImage.subscribe(
30        imageData => {
31          this.imageInfo = imageData;
32          this.imageHistory.push(imageData);
33        });
34    }
35  }
```

Listing 11.10 shows an Angular template that displays a random image in the main view. `ngFor` is used to display each image within the image history array.

Listing 11.10 `app.component.html`: **An Angular Template that Displays Images Emitted from** `RandomImageService`

```
01 <div>
02   <img src="{{imageInfo.url}}"
03        width="{{imageInfo.width}}">
04   <p>{{imageInfo.title}}</p>
05 </div>
06 <hr>
07 <h3>Random Image History</h3>
08 <span *ngFor = "let image of imageHistory">
09   <img src="{{image.url}}" height="50px">
10 </span>
```

Listing 11.11 shows a CSS file that styles the application with a border for the main image and text.

Listing 11.11 `app.component.css`: **A CSS File that Styles the Application Separating the Main View from the Smaller Pictures**

```
01 div {
02     position: inline-block;
03     width: fit-content;
04     border: 3px solid black;
05 }
```

```
06 p {
07     font: bold 25px 'Times New Roman';
08     padding: 5px;
09     text-align: center;
10 }
```

Figure 11.3 shows the running example. The main image URL and size are randomly changed by the service. A rolling history of the randomly displayed images is shown at the bottom.

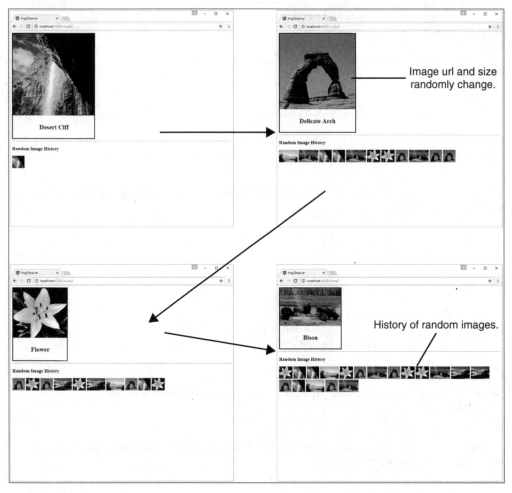

Figure 11.3   Implementing a variable data service that updates a component with random changes to image size and URL

Implementing a Service that Returns a Promise

This example shows how to build a service that creates and returns a promise.

Listing 11.12 shows a custom service named `PromiseService`, which creates an asynchronous timer that alerts the user after a particular number of seconds. Lines 6 through 13 define the method `createTimedAlert`, which takes in the parameter `seconds` and returns a promise. Lines 8 through 10 create a `resolve` function, which runs only after the promise completes. This function creates an alert that tells the user how long it took to run the alert.

Listing 11.12   `promise.service.ts`: **An Angular Service that Provides a Timer-Based Alert**

```
01 Import { Injectable } from '@angular/core';
02
03 @Injectable()
04 export class PromiseService {
05
06   createTimedAlert(seconds: number): Promise<any>{
07     return new Promise((resolve, reject) =>{
08       resolve(setTimeout(function(){
09           alert('this alert took ' + seconds + ' seconds to load');
10         }, (seconds * 1000))
11       );
12     })
13   }
```

Listing 11.13 shows an Angular component that uses `PromiseService` to create an asynchronous request that can be resolved at a later time. Lines 2 and 7 show `PromiseService` being imported and then added to the `providers` array so it is available to the component. Line 12 creates an instance of `PromiseService` called `alert`. Lines 15 through 17 define the `createAlert` method, which invokes the `createtimedAlert` method on `alert` and passes in the `seconds` variable.

Listing 11.13   `app.component.ts`: **An Angular Component that Uses the** `PromiseService` **Service**

```
01 import { Component } from '@angular/core';
02 import { PromiseService } from './promise.service';
03
04 @Component({
05   selector: 'app-root',
06   templateUrl: './app.component.html',
07   providers: [PromiseService]
08 })
09 export class AppComponent {
10   seconds: number = 0;
```

```
11   constructor(
12     private alert: PromiseService
13   ){}
14
15   createAlert(){
16     this.alert.createTimedAlert(this.seconds);
17   }
18 }
```

Listing 11.14 shows an Angular template that has an input the user can use to type the amount of time in seconds. The template has a button that invokes the function `createAlert`.

Listing 11.14 `app.component.htm`: **A Template that Displays a Button to Start the Asynchronous Alert Request**

```
01 <h3>set the time in seconds to create an alert</h3>
02 <input [(ngModel)]="seconds">
03 <button (click)="createAlert()">go</button>
```

Figure 11.4 shows the asynchronous alert being displayed by the service after the time has elapsed.

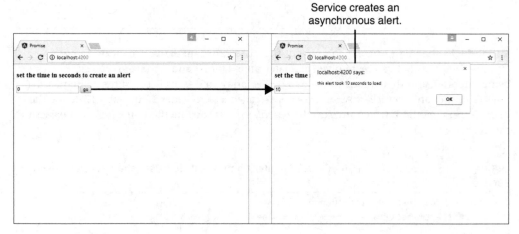

Figure 11.4 Using an Angular service to provide asynchronous alerts

Implementing a Shared Service

This example shows how to build a service that is shared between two components. There will only be one instance of this service, which means that when one component changes the data, the other component will see that data change as well.

Listing 11.15 shows a custom service named SharedService, which creates an observable of an array of characters. This observable is editable, which makes it useful for reducing characters' health. When the values are changed, the observable emits that change to all components that are subscribed to the observable.

Lines15 through 52 define the characters array, which contains the values name, race, alignment, and health. Lines 55 through 60 define the constructor method, which creates the observable charObservable. The observer object is saved to the service variable observer. Then the observer emits the characters array. Lines 62 through 64 define the getCharacters method, which returns the charObservable.

Lines 66 through 79 define the hitCharacter method, which takes two parameters: character and damage. The method then searches for the index of character within the characters array. If the character exists in the array, the method subtracts damage from that character's health. Then if the health is less than or equal to 0, the method removes the character from the array. Finally, the method emits the updated characters array.

Listing 11.15   shared.service.ts: **An Angular Service that Will Be Shared Between Components**

```
01 import { Injectable } from '@angular/core';
02
03 import { Observable }     from 'rxjs/Observable';
04 import 'rxjs';
05
06 export class character {
07   name: string;
08   race: string;
09   alignment: string;
10   health: number;
11 }
12
13 @Injectable()
14 export class SharedService{
15 characters: character[] = [
16      {
17         name: 'Aragon',
18         race: 'human',
19         alignment: 'good',
20         health: 100
21      },
22      {
23         name: 'Legolas',
24         race: 'elf',
25         alignment: 'good',
26         health: 100
27      },
28      {
29         name: 'Gimli',
```

```
30              race: 'Dwarf',
31              alignment: 'good',
32              health: 100
33          },
34          {
35            name: 'Witch King',
36            race: 'Wraith',
37            alignment: 'bad',
38            health: 100
39          },
40          {
41            name: 'Lurtz',
42            race: 'Uruk-hai',
43            alignment: 'bad',
44            health: 100
45          },
46          {
47            name: 'Sarumon',
48            race: 'Wizard',
49            alignment: 'bad',
50            health: 100
51          },
52      ];
53    charObservable: Observable<character[]>;
54    observer;
55    constructor(){
56      this.charObservable = new Observable(observer => {
57        this.observer = observer;
58        this.observer.next(this.characters);
59      })
60    }
61
62    getCharacters(): Observable<character[]>{
63      return this.charObservable;
64    }
65
66    hitCharacter(character, damage){
67
68      var index = this.characters.indexOf(character, 0);
69        if(index > -1){
70          this.characters[index].health -= damage;
71          if(this.characters[index].health <= 0){
72              this.characters.splice(index, 1);
73          }
74        }
75      this.observer.next(this.characters);
76    }
77 }
```

Listing 11.16 shows an Angular component that creates a single instance of `SharedService` that can be passed down to child components. Because each child receives the same instance of the service, all child components that inject the `SharedService` and subscribe to its observable will be updated anytime the data changes. Lines 2 and 7 import and provide `SharedService` for use within the component. Line 11 assigns `SharedService` to the variable `shared` to be used within the HTML.

Listing 11.16 `app.component.ts`: **An Angular Component that Distributes** `SharedService`

```
01 import { Component } from '@angular/core';
02 import { SharedService } from './shared.service';
03
04 @Component({
05   selector: 'app-root',
06   templateUrl: './app.component.html',
07   providers: [ SharedService ]
08 })
09 export class AppComponent {
10   constructor(
11      public shared: SharedService
12   ){}
13 }
```

Listing 11.17 shows an Angular template that displays two sections: one for good guys one for bad guys. Line 2 shows the Good Guys component, which takes in an input `shared` and is passed the `shared` observable from `app.component` to `good-guys.component`. Line 5 shows the Bad Guys component, which takes in an input `shared` and is passed the `shared` observable from `app.component` to `badguys.component`.

Listing 11.17 `app.component.html`: **An Angular Template File that Distributes** `SharedService` **to Two Components**

```
01 <h2>Good Guys</h2>
02 <app-good-guys [shared]="shared"></app-good-guys>
03   <hr>
04 <h2>Bad Guys</h2>
05 <app-badguys [shared]="shared"></app-badguys>
```

Listing 11.18 shows the Angular component `good-guys.component`. Line 9 shows the input `shared` that gets the `SharedService` observable from `app.component`. Lines 14 through 16 show `getCharacters` being subscribed to on the `shared` service; this sets the variable `characters` to the emitted value from the observable returned from the method. Lines 18 through 20 define the `hitCharacter` method, which takes two parameters: `character` and `damage`. This method calls the `hitCharacter` method on the shared service and passes in `character` and `damage` as parameters.

Listing 11.18 `good-guys.component.ts`: **An Angular Component that Watches and Displays a Shared Observable**

```
01 import { Component, OnInit, Input } from '@angular/core';
02
03 @Component({
04   selector: 'app-good-guys',
05   templateUrl: './good-guys.component.html',
06   styleUrls: ['./good-guys.component.css']
07 })
08 export class GoodGuysComponent implements OnInit {
09   @Input('shared') shared;
10   characters: Array<any>;
11   constructor(){}
12
13   ngOnInit(){
14     this.shared.getCharacters().subscribe(
15       characters => this.characters = characters
16     );
17   }
18   hitCharacter(character, damage){
19     this.shared.hitCharacter(character, damage)
20   }
21 }
```

Listing 11.19 shows an Angular template that displays a list of characters. Lines 3 through 5 display the character's name, race, and health. Lines 6 through 8 show that characters with the alignment `'bad'` have a button that invokes the `hitCharacter` method which takes in the `character` object and the number 25 as parameters.

Listing 11.19 `good-guys.component.html`: **An Angular Template that Displays a List of Characters**

```
01 <div *ngFor="let character of characters">
02   <div class="character">
03       <b>Name:</b> {{character.name}}<br>
04       <b>Race:</b> {{character.race}}<br>
05       <b>Health:</b> {{character.health}}
06     <span *ngIf="character.alignment == 'bad'">
07       <button (click)="hitCharacter(character, 25)">hit</button>
08     </span>
09   </div>
10 </div>
```

Listing 11.20 shows a CSS file that adds borders to each character to help distinguish the characters as separate entities.

Listing 11.20 `good-guys.component.css`: **A CSS File that Visually Separates Characters into Their Own Cards**

```css
01 b{
02   font-weight: bold;
03 }
04 div {
05   display: inline-block;
06   margin: 10px;
07   padding: 5px;
08 }
09 .character {
10   border: 2px solid steelblue;
11 }
```

Listing 11.21 shows the Angular component `badguys.component`. Line 10 shows the input `shared` that gets the `SharedService` observable from `app.component`. Lines 15 through 17 show `getCharacters` being subscribed to on the `shared` service; this sets the variable `characters` to the emitted value from the observable returned from the method. Lines 19 through 21 define the `hitCharacter` method, which takes two parameters: `character` and `damage`. This method calls the `hitCharacter` method on the shared service to pass in `character` and `damage` as parameters.

Listing 11.21 `badguys.component.ts`: **An Angular Component that Watches and Displays a Shared Observable**

```typescript
01 import { Component, OnInit, Input } from '@angular/core';
02
03 @Component({
04   selector: 'app-badguys',
05   templateUrl: './badguys.component.html',
06   styleUrls: ['./badguys.component.css']
07 })
08
09 export class BadguysComponent implements OnInit {
10   @Input('shared') shared;
11   characters: Array<any>;
12   constructor(){ }
13
14   ngOnInit(){
15     this.shared.getCharacters().subscribe(
16         characters => this.characters = characters
17     );
18   }
19   hitCharacter(character, damage){
20     this.shared.hitCharacter(character, damage);
21   }
22 }
```

Listing 11.22 shows an Angular template that displays a list of characters. Lines 3 through 5 display the character's name, race, and health. Lines 6 through 8 show that characters with the alignment 'good' also have a button that invokes the hitCharacter method to which takes in the character object and 25 as parameters.

Listing 11.22 `badguys.component.html`: **An Angular Template that Displays a List of Characters**

```
01 <div *ngFor="let character of characters">
02   <div class="character">
03     <b>Name:</b> {{character.name}}<br>
04     <b>Race:</b> {{character.race}}<br>
05     <b>Health:</b> {{character.health}}
06     <span *ngIf="character.alignment == 'good'">
07       <button (click)="hitCharacter(character, 25)">hit</button>
08     </span>
09   </div>
10 </div>
```

Listing 11.23 shows a CSS file that adds borders to each character to help distinguish the character as separate entities.

Listing 11.23 `badguys.component.css`: **A CSS File that Visually Separates Characters into Their Own Cards**

```
01 b{
02   font-weight: bold;
03 }
04 div {
05   display: inline-block;
06   margin: 10px;
07   padding: 5px;
08 }
09 .character {
10   border: 2px solid steelblue;
11 }
```

Figure 11.5 shows the application that connects a Good Guys component with a Bad Guys component. Clicking the hit button updates the shared service, which is observed by both components.

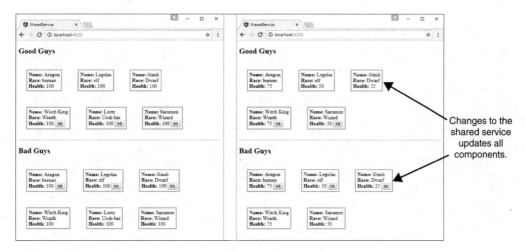

Figure 11.5   Using a shared Angular service to update multiple components

Summary

Angular custom services provide functionality that can be injected into other Angular services and components. Services allow you to organize your code into functional modules that can be used to create libraries of functionality available to Angular applications.

This chapter focuses on tools that enable you to implement your own custom Angular services for providing task-based functionality to applications. This chapter provides examples of implementing each of various types of custom Angular services.

Having Fun with Angular

Angular provides a lot of functionality and is a well-featured framework. The previous chapters in this book have given you everything you need to understand what Angular has to offer. This chapter is a bit different from the previous ones. It provides some additional examples that expand on what you have learned so far. The examples in this chapter take bits and pieces from all the previous chapters and show you how to build fun and useful applications that demonstrate more of what Angular is capable of.

Implementing an Angular Application that Uses the Animation Service

Listings 12.1 through 12.6 show how to create an Angular application that uses the animation service to animate images. An image fades in and grows to the correct size when the mouse hovers over the image title. When the mouse leaves, the image shrinks and fades out of view.

The folder structure for this example is as follows:

- `./app.module.ts`: App module that imports animations (see Listing 12.1)

- `./app.component.ts`: Angular root component for the application (see Listing 12.2)

- `./app.component.html`: Angular template file for `app.component` (see Listing 12.3)

- `./animated`: Animated component folder

- `./animated/animated.component.ts`: Angular component that handles animations (see Listing 12.4)

- `./animated/animated.component.html`: Angular template for the `animated` component (see Listing 12.5)

- `./animated/animated.component.css`: CSS file for the `animated` component (see Listing 12.6)

Listing 12.1 shows the application module. For the application to use the animation service, `BrowserAnimationsModule` needs to be loaded. Lines 3 and 15 show `BrowserAnimationsModule` being imported from `@angular/platform-browser/animations` and then added to the `imports` array to make animations available to the application.

Listing 12.1   `app.module.ts`: **An Angular Module that Includes** `BrowserAnimationsModule`

```
01 import { BrowserModule } from '@angular/platform-browser';
02 import { NgModule } from '@angular/core';
03 import { BrowserAnimationsModule } from
04 '@angular/platform-browser/animations';
05
06 import { AppComponent } from './app.component';
07 import { AnimatedComponent } from './animated/animated.component';
08
09 @NgModule({
10   declarations: [
11     AppComponent,
12     AnimatedComponent
13   ],
14   imports: [
15     BrowserModule,
16     BrowserAnimationsModule
17   ],
18   providers: [],
19   bootstrap: [AppComponent]
20 })
21 export class AppModule { }
```

Listing 12.2 shows an Angular component that acts as the root of the application. This component loads a template file that uses the `animated` component.

Listing 12.2   `app.component.ts`: **An Angular Component that Acts as the Root to the Application**

```
01 import { Component } from '@angular/core';
02 import { AnimatedComponent } from './animated/animated.component';
03
04 @Component({
05   selector: 'app-root',
06   templateUrl: './app.component.html'
07 })
08 export class AppComponent {}
```

Listing 12.3 shows an Angular template that loads the `animated` component four times and passes in an image URL to the input `src`. It also adds a title to the input `title`.

Listing 12.3   `app.component.html`: **An Angular Template that Uses the** `animated`
Component

```
01 <animated title="Arch"
02          src="../../assets/images/arch.jpg">
03 </animated>
04 <animated title="Volcano"
05          src="../../assets/images/volcano.jpg">
06 </animated>
07 <animated title="Flower"
08          src="../../assets/images/flower.jpg">
09 </animated>
10 <animated title="Sunset"
11          src="../../assets/images/jump.jpg">
12 </animated>
```

Listing 12.4 shows an Angular `animated` component which handles the animation of an image that is passed in via an input. Lines 1 through 3 import `animate`, `keyframes`, `state`, `style`, `transition`, and `trigger` from `@angular/core` to make animations for this application possible.

Lines 9 through 36 define the animations metadata for the component. Lines 10 through 23 show the trigger for the animation called `fadeState`, which when activated calls two states, `inactive` and `active`, and two transitions, `inactive => active` (which creates a 500 ms `ease-in` animation) and `active => inactive` (which creates a 500 ms `ease-out` animation).

Lines 24 through 34 show the trigger `bounceState`, which contains the transition `void => *`. This transition creates an animation that causes the menu items to bounce down and up when the application is first loaded. Lines 45 through 47 define the `enter` method, which sets the variable `state` to `active`. Lines 48 and 49 define the `leave` method, which sets the variable `state` to `inactive`.

Listing 12.4   `animated.component.ts`: **An Angular Component that Uses the**
Animation Service

```
01 import { Component, OnInit, Input,
02          animate, keyframes, state,
03          style, transition, trigger } from '@angular/core';
04
05 @Component({
06   selector: 'animated',
07   templateUrl: './animated.component.html',
08   styleUrls: ['./animated.component.css'],
09   animations: [
10     trigger('fadeState', [
11       state('inactive', style({
12         transform: 'scale(.5) translateY(-50%)',
```

```
13          opacity: 0
14      })),
15      state('active', style({
16        transform: 'scale(1) translateY(0)',
17        opacity: 1
18      })),
19      transition('inactive => active',
20                  animate('500ms ease-in')),
21      transition('active => inactive',
22                  animate('500ms ease-out'))
23    ]),
24    trigger('bounceState', [
25      transition('void => *', [
26        animate(600, keyframes([
27          style({ opacity: 0,
28                  transform: 'translateY(-50px)' }),
29          style({ opacity: .5,
30                  transform: 'translateY(50px)' }),
31          style({ opacity: 1,
32                  transform: 'translateY(0)' }),
33        ]))
34      ])
35    ])
36  ]
37 })
38 export class AnimatedComponent implements OnInit {
39   @Input ("src") src: string;
40   @Input ("title") title: string;
41   state: string = 'inactive';
42   constructor() { }
43   ngOnInit() {
44   }
45   enter(){
46     this.state = 'active';
47   }
48   leave(){
49     this.state = 'inactive';
50   }
51 }
```

Listing 12.5 shows an Angular template that displays a title and an image. Line 1 shows the Angular animation @bounceState being used; it is passed in the variable state from the component to determine what animation sequence should be used. Lines 7 and 8 show @fadeState being implemented; it also has state passed in to determine the animation sequence.

Listing 12.5 `animated.Component.html`: **An Angular Template That Displays Image Titles with Images That Are Animated**

```
01 <div [@bounceState]='state'>
02   <p
03     (mouseenter)="enter()"
04     (mouseleave)="leave()">
05   {{title}}
06   </p>
07   <img src="{{src}}"
08       [@fadeState]='state' />
09 </div>
```

Listing 12.6 shows a CSS file that styles the titles for the images and sets the dimensions for the images.

Listing 12.6 `animated.component.css`: **A CSS File That Styles the** `animated` **Component**

```
01 div {
02   display: inline-block;
03   padding: 0px;
04   margin: 0px;
05 }
06 p {
07   font: bold 16px/30px Times New Roman;
08   color: #226bd8;
09   border: 1px solid lightblue;
10   background: linear-gradient(white, lightblue, skyblue);
11   text-align: center;
12   padding: 0px;
13   margin: 0px;
14   vertical-align: top;
15 }
16 img {
17   width: 150px;
18   vertical-align: top;
19 }
```

Figure 12.1 shows how the images animate in size and opacity when you click on the image name.

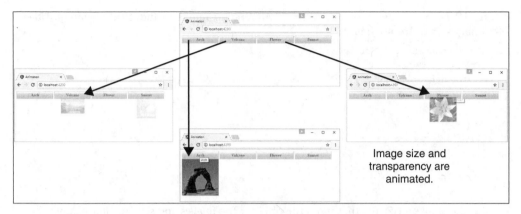

Figure 12.1   Using Angular's built-in animation service to animate images

Implementing an Angular Application that Zooms in on Images

Listings 12.7 through 12.12 show you how to create an Angular application that displays images that can be zoomed in on (via browser events) when they are clicked.

The folder structure for this example is as follows:

- **./app/app.component.ts:** Root component for the application (see Listing 12.7)

- **./app/app.component.html:** Angular template for the root component (see Listing 12.8)

- **./app/zoomit:** Folder containing the zoomit component

- **./app/zoomit/zoomit.component.ts:** Angular component called zoomit (see Listing 12.9)

- **./app/zoomit/zoomit.component.html:** Angular template for the zoomit component (see Listing 12.10)

- **./app/zoomit/zoomit.component.html:** CSS file for the zoomit component (see Listing 12.11)

- **./assets/images:** Folder where the image files for the example will be kept

Listing 12.7 shows an Angular component that acts as the root of the application. This component loads a template file that uses the zoomit component.

Listing 12.7   `app.component.ts`: **An Angular Component That Acts as the Root to the Application**

```
01 import { Component } from '@angular/core';
02 import { ZoomitComponent } from './zoomit/zoomit.component';
03
04 @Component({
05   selector: 'app-root',
06   templateUrl: './app.component.html'
07 })
08 export class AppComponent {}
```

Listing 12.8 shows an Angular template that creates three `zoomit` components by passing in the image URL as the attribute `zsrc`.

Listing 12.8   `app.component.html`: **An Angular Template That Implements the Component** `zoomit`

```
01 <hr>
02 <zoomit zsrc="../../assets/images/volcano.jpg"></zoomit>
03 <hr>
04 <zoomit zsrc="../../assets/images/flower2.jpg"></zoomit>
05 <hr>
06 <zoomit zsrc="../../assets/images/arch.jpg"></zoomit>
07 <hr>
```

Listing 12.9 shows the Angular `zoomit` component, which handles zooming in on a section of an image by using browser events. Lines 13 through 16 define the `ngOnInit` method, which generates a URL to get an image based on the name of the image passed into the component via the `zsrc` input. `ngOnInit` then sets a default position. Lines 18 through 23 define the `imageClick` event, which takes in a parameter `event`. Then it gets the element from the `event` object and uses that to set new x and y coordinates as the basis for the zoom of the image.

Listing 12.9   `zoomit.component.ts`: **An Angular Component That Uses Browser Events to Zoom In on Part of an Image**

```
01 import { Component, OnInit, Input } from '@angular/core';
02
03 @Component({
04   selector: 'zoomit',
05   templateUrl: './zoomit.component.html',
06   styleUrls: ['./zoomit.component.css']
07 })
08 export class ZoomitComponent implements OnInit {
09   @Input("zsrc") zsrc: string;
10   public pos: string;
```

```
11    public zUrl: string;
12
13    ngOnInit() {
14      this.zUrl = 'url("' + this.zsrc + '")';
15      this.pos = "50% 50%";
16    }
17
18    imageClick(event: any){
19      let element = event.target;
20      let posX = Math.ceil(event.offsetX/element.width * 100);
21      let posY = Math.ceil(event.offsetY/element.height * 100);
22      this.pos = posX +"% " + posY + "%";
23    }
24  }
```

Listing 12.10 shows an Angular template that displays an image and a zoomed in portion of the image next to it, using the coordinates generated from the `imageClick` function.

Listing 12.10 `zoomit.component.html`: **An Angular Template That Displays an Image as Well as a Zoomed In Portion of That Image**

```
01 <img src="{{zsrc}}" (click)="imageClick($event)"/>
02 <div class="zoombox"
03      [style.background-image]="zUrl"
04      [style.background-position]="pos">
05 </div>
```

Listing 12.11 shows a CSS file that styles the application by adding a border to the zoomed in image. It also sets `width` and `height` to `100px`.

Listing 12.11 `zoomit.component.css`: **A CSS File That Styles the Application**

```
01 img {
02    width: 200px;
03 }
04 .zoombox {
05    display: inline-block;
06    border: 3px ridge black;
07    width: 100px;
08    height: 100px;
09    background-repeat: no-repeat;
10 }
```

Figure 12.2 shows how the custom component displays a zoomed in portion of the image. When you click on the image, the position of the zoom is changed.

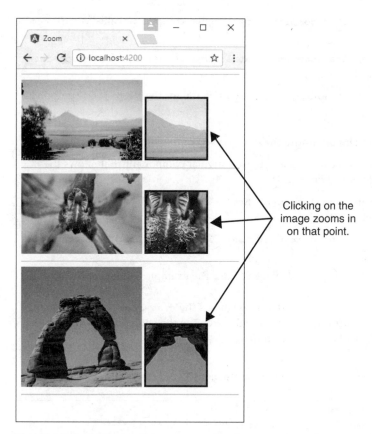

Clicking on the image zooms in on that point.

Figure 12.2   Implementing a custom Angular component that zooms in on a portion of an image

Implementing an Angular Application that Enables Drag and Drop

Listings 12.12 through 12.20 show how to create an Angular application that displays images that can have descriptive tags dragged and dropped onto them.

The folder structure for this example is as follows:

- **./app/app.component.ts:** Root component for the application (see Listing 12.12)

- **./app/app.component.html:** Angular template for the `root` component (see Listing 12.13)

- **./app/app.component.css:** CSS file for `app.component` (see Listing 12.14)

- **./app/drop-item:** Folder containing the `drop-item` component

- ./app/drop-item/drop-item.component.ts: Angular component called drop-item (see Listing 12.15)

- ./app/drop-item/drop-item.component.html: Angular template for the drop-item component (see Listing 12.16)

- ./app/drop-item/drop-item.component.css: CSS file for the drop-item component (see Listing 12.17)

- ./app/drag-item: Folder containing the drag-item component

- ./app/drag-item/drop-item.component.ts: Angular component that allows the dragging of an element (see Listing 12.18)

- ./app/drag-item/drop-item.component.html: Angular template for the drag-item component (see Listing 12.19)

- ./app/drag-item/drop-item.component.css: CSS file for the drag-item component (see Listing 12.20)

- ./assets/images: Folder where the image files for the example will be kept

Listing 12.12 shows an Angular component that implements the drag-item and drop-item components to apply tags to images. Lines 12 through 24 define the constructor, which initializes a list of tags available to be dragged onto an image.

Listing 12.12 app.component.ts: **An Angular Component That Acts as the Root to the Application**

```
01 import { Component } from '@angular/core';
02 import { DragItemComponent} from './drag-item/drag-item.component';
03 import { DropItemComponent} from './drop-item/drop-item.component';
04
05 @Component({
06   selector: 'app-root',
07   templateUrl: './app.component.html',
08   styleUrls: ['./app.component.css']
09 })
10 export class AppComponent {
11   tagList: string[];
12   constructor() {
13     this.tagList = [
14       'Nature',
15       'Landscape',
16       'Flora',
17       'Sunset',
18       'Desert',
19       'Beauty',
20       'Inspiring',
21       'Summer',
```

```
22      'Fun'
23    ]
24   }
25   ngOnInit() {
26    }
27 }
```

Listing 12.13 shows an Angular template that implements the `drag-item` and `drop-item` components, which allow tags to be dragged and dropped onto images.

Listing 12.13 `app.component.html`: **An Angular Template That Implements the** `drag-item` **and** `drop-item` **Components**

```
01 <h1>Tagging Images</h1>
02 <hr>
03 <div class="tagBox">
04     <span *ngFor="let tagText of tagList">
05         <drag-item [tag]="tagText"></drag-item>
06     </span>
07 </div>
08 <hr>
09
10 <drop-item
11 [imgsrc]="'../../assets/images/arch.jpg'">
12 </drop-item>
13 <drop-item
14 [imgsrc]="'../../assets/images/lake.jpg'">
15 </drop-item>
16 <drop-item
17 [imgsrc]="'../../assets/images/jump.jpg'">
18 </drop-item>
19 <drop-item
20 [imgsrc]="'../../assets/images/flower.jpg'">
21 </drop-item>
22 <drop-item
23 [imgsrc]="'../../assets/images/volcano.jpg'">
24 </drop-item>
```

Listing 12.14 shows a CSS file that styles the application to give direct styles to the `drop-item` custom HTML tag.

Listing 12.14 `app.component.css`: **A CSS File That Styles the Application**

```
01 .tagBox {
02   width: 320px;
03   padding: 5px;
04 }
```

```
05 drop-item{
06    display: inline-block;
07    vertical-align: top;
08    margin-bottom: 5px;
09 }
```

Listing 12.15 shows the Angular component drop-item, which uses browser events to allow an element to be dropped onto the component element. Lines 11 through 13 define the constructor that initializes the tags variable as an empty array.

Lines 16 through 18 define the allowDrop method, which takes an event object as a parameter. The preventDefault method is invoked on the event object. Lines 19 through 25 define the onDrop method, which takes in an event object as a parameter. preventDefault is called on the event object. Then the variable data is assigned tagData from the event to allow Angular to add that data to the tags array and to the list on the image.

Listing 12.15 drop.component.ts: **An Angular Component That Allows for an Item to Be Dropped on the Element**

```
01 import { Component, OnInit, Input } from '@angular/core';
02
03 @Component({
04    selector: 'drop-item',
05    templateUrl: './drop-item.component.html',
06    styleUrls: ['./drop-item.component.css']
07 })
08 export class DropItemComponent implements OnInit {
09    @Input() imgsrc: string;
10    tags: string[];
11    constructor() {
12      this.tags = [];
13    }
14    ngOnInit() {
15    }
16    allowDrop(event) {
17      event.preventDefault();
18    }
19    onDrop(event) {
20      event.preventDefault();
21      let data = JSON.parse(event.dataTransfer.getData('tagData'));
22      if (!this.tags.includes(data.tag)){
23        this.tags.push(data.tag);
24      }
25    }
26 }
```

Listing 12.16 shows an Angular template that displays an image and any tags assigned to that image.

Listing 12.16 `drop.component.html`: **An Angular Template That Displays an Image and Any Image Tags Dropped onto That Image**

```
01 <div class="taggedImage"
02     (dragover)="allowDrop($event)"
03     (drop)="onDrop($event)">
04   <img src="{{imgsrc}}" />
05   <span class="imageTag"
06        *ngFor="let tag of tags">
07   {{tag}}
08   </span>
09 </div>
```

Listing 12.17 shows a CSS file that styles the application by adding custom styles to the tags attached to the image.

Listing 12.17 `drop.component.css`: **A CSS File That Styles the Application**

```
01 img{
02     width: 100px;
03 }
04 .taggedImage{
05     display: inline-block;
06     width: 100px;
07     background: #000000;
08 }
09 .imageTag {
10     display: inline-block;
11     width: 100px;
12     font: 16px/18px Georgia, serif;
13     text-align: center;
14     color: white;
15     background: linear-gradient(#888888, #000000);
16 }
```

Listing 12.18 shows the Angular component `drag-item`, which uses browser events to allow elements to be dragged. Lines 14 through 17 define the `onDrag` method, which takes an `event` object as a parameter. This method adds data to the `dataTransfer` item on the `event` object to allow the tag data to be transferred when the element is dropped.

Listing 12.18 `drag.component.ts`: **An Angular Component That Allows an Element to Be Dragged**

```
01 import { Component, OnInit, Input } from '@angular/core';
02
03 @Component({
04   selector: 'drag-item',
05   templateUrl: './drag-item.component.html',
06   styleUrls: ['./drag-item.component.css']
07 })
08 export class DragItemComponent implements OnInit {
09   @Input() tag: string;
10   constructor() {
11   }
12   ngOnInit() {
13   }
14   onDrag(event) {
15     event.dataTransfer.setData('tagData',
16         JSON.stringify({tag: this.tag}));
17   }
18 }
```

Listing 12.19 shows an Angular template that displays a draggable tag.

Listing 12.19 `drag.component.html`: **An Angular Template That Displays an Image Tag**

```
01 <div class="tagItem"
02     (dragstart)="onDrag($event)"
03     draggable="true">
04   {{tag}}
05 </div>
```

Listing 12.20 shows a CSS file that styles the application by adding custom styles to the tags.

Listing 12.20 `drag.component.css`: **A CSS File That Styles the Application**

```
01 .tagItem {
02    display: inline-block;
03    width: 100px;
04    font: 16px/18px Georgia, serif;
05    text-align: center;
06    background: linear-gradient(#FFFFFF, #888888);
07 }
```

Figure 12.3 shows how the `drag-item` and `drop-item` components work in a browser: When you drag a tag onto an image, the tag is added to the list below.

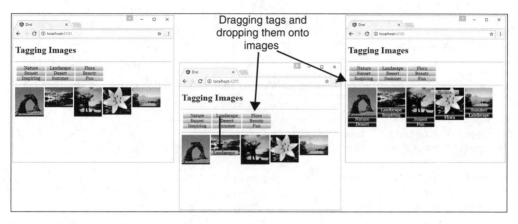

Dragging tags and dropping them onto images

Figure 12.3   Implementing drag and drop using Angular components

Implementing a Star Rating Angular Component

Listings 12.22 through 12.30 show how to create an Angular application that creates a star rating system so a user can give ratings to items attached to the component (images in this case).

The folder structure for this example is as follows:

- **./app/app.module.ts:** Root component for the application (see Listing 12.21)

- **./app/mockbackend.service.ts:** Angular template for the root component (see Listing 12.22)

- **./app/app.module.ts:** CSS file for app.component (see Listing 12.23)

- **./app/app.component.ts:** Root component for the application (see Listing 12.24)

- **./app/app.component.html:** Angular template for the root component (see Listing 12.25)

- **./app/app.component.css:** CSS file for app.component (see Listing 12.26)

- **./app/rated-item:** Folder containing the rated-item component.

- **./app/rated-item/rated-item.component.ts:** Angular component that lets the user rate items (see Listing 12.27)

- **./app/rated-item/rated-item.component.html:** Angular template for the rated-item component (see Listing 12.28)

- **./app/rated-item/rated-item.component.css:** CSS file for the rated-item component (see Listing 12.29)

Listing 12.21 shows the application module. This module uses `InMemoryWebApiModule`, which allows for the creation of a mock database. Line 18 shows the implementation of `InMemoryWebApiModule`.

Listing 12.21   `app.module.ts`: **An Angular Module That Implements** `InMemoryWebApiModule`

```
01 import { BrowserModule } from '@angular/platform-browser';
02 import { NgModule } from '@angular/core';
03 import { HttpModule } from '@angular/http';
04 import { InMemoryWebApiModule } from 'angular-in-memory-web-api';
05
06 import { AppComponent } from './app.component';
07 import { RatedItemComponent } from './rated-item/rated-item.component';
08 import { MockbackendService } from './mockbackend.service';
09
10 @NgModule({
11   declarations: [
12     AppComponent,
13     RatedItemComponent
14   ],
15   imports: [
16     BrowserModule,
17     HttpModule,
18     InMemoryWebApiModule.forRoot(MockbackendService)
19   ],
20   providers: [],
21   bootstrap: [AppComponent]
22 })
23 export class AppModule { }
```

Listing 12.22 shows an Angular service that acts as a mock database for the application. Lines 4 through 29 create an array of items that can be retrieved and updated via HTTP requests.

Listing 12.22   `mockbackend.service.ts`: **An Angular Mock Back-end Service**

```
01 import { InMemoryDbService } from 'angular-in-memory-web-api';
02 export class MockbackendService implements InMemoryDbService{
03   createDb() {
04     const items = [
05       {
06         id: 1,
07         title: "Waterfall",
08         url: "../../assets/images/cliff.jpg",
09         rating: 4
10       },
11       {
```

```
12           id: 2,
13           title: "Flower",
14           url: "../../assets/images/flower.jpg",
15           rating: 5
16         },
17         {
18           id: 3,
19           title: "Pyramid",
20           url: "../../assets/images/pyramid.jpg",
21           rating: 3
22         },
23         {
24           id: 4,
25           title: "Lake",
26           url: "../../assets/images/lake.jpg",
27           rating: 5
28         }
29       ]
30     return {items};
31   }
32 }
```

Listing 12.23 shows an Angular service that uses HTTP to retrieve and update the items in the mock database. Lines 6 through 11 define the `RatedItem` interface with strictly typed variable names. Lines 19 through 24 define the constructor that creates an instance of `http` and a new observable called `itemObservable`.

Once a response is received from the observable, the `getItems` method is called. Lines 27 and 28 define the `getObservable` method, which returns `itemObservable`. Lines 30 through 38 define the `getItems` method, which uses an HTTP `get` to retrieve the items list from the mock database; it then assigns the `items` variable to the response and emits that response to the observer.

Lines 39 through 47 define the `updateRating` method, which takes two parameters: `item` and `newRating`. It assigns the item rating `newRating` and uses an HTTP `put` request to update the item in the database.

Listing 12.23 `ratings.service.ts`: **An Angular Service That Uses HTTP to Retrieve a List of Items with Ratings**

```
01 import { Injectable, OnInit } from '@angular/core';
02 import { Http }        from '@angular/http';
03 import { Observable } from 'rxjs/observable';
04 import 'rxjs/add/operator/toPromise';
05
06 export class RatedItem {
07   id: number;
```

```
08   url: string;
09   title: string;
10   rating: number;
11 }
12
13 @Injectable()
14 export class RatingsService {
15   url = 'api/items';
16   items: RatedItem[];
17   public itemObservable: Observable<any>;
18   observer;
19   constructor(private http: Http) {
20     this.itemObservable = new Observable(observer => {
21       this.observer = observer;
22       this.getItems();
23     })
24   }
25   ngOnInit(){
26   }
27   getObservable(){
28     return this.itemObservable;
29   }
30   getItems(){
31     this.http.get(this.url)
32             .toPromise()
33             .then( response => {
34               this.items = response.json().data;
35               this.observer.next(this.items);
36             })
37             .catch(this.handleError);
38   }
39   updateRating(item, newRating){
40     item.rating = newRating;
41     const url = `${this.url}/${item.id}`;
42     this.http
43       .put(url, JSON.stringify(item))
44       .toPromise()
45       .then(() => this.getItems())
46       .catch(this.handleError)
47   }
48   private handleError(error: any): Promise<any> {
49     console.error('An error occurred', error);
50     return Promise.reject(error.message || error);
51   }
52 }
```

Listing 12.24 shows an Angular component that handles getting the items from
`RatingsService`. Lines 21 through 27 define `ngOnInit`, which invokes the `getObservable`
method on `ratingsService` to assign the `items` observable to `itemsObservable`. The `items`
variable is then assigned the response received from `itemsObservable`.

Listing 12.24   `app.component.ts`: An Angular Component That Acts as the Root to the Application

```
01 import { Component } from '@angular/core';
02 import { RatedItemComponent } from './rated-item/rated-item.component';
03 import { Observable } from 'rxjs/observable';
04 import { RatingsService } from './ratings.service';
05
06 @Component({
07   selector: 'app-root',
08   templateUrl: './app.component.html',
09   styleUrls: ['./app.component.css'],
10   providers: [ RatingsService ]
11 })
12 export class AppComponent {
13   title = 'app';
14   itemsObservable: Observable<any>;
15   items: any[];
16   constructor(
17     public ratingsService: RatingsService
18   ){
19     this.items = [];
20   }
21   ngOnInit(){
22     this.itemsObservable = this.ratingsService.getObservable();
23     this.itemsObservable.subscribe(
24       itemList => {
25         this.items = itemList;
26       });
27   }
28 }
```

Listing 12.25 shows an Angular template that implements the `rated-item` component to
display a list of rated items. `rated-item` takes two inputs: `item` and `ratingsService`.

Listing 12.25   `app.component.html`: An Angular Template That Creates a List of Rated Items, Using the Component `rated-item`

```
01 <h1> Rated Images </h1>
02 <hr>
03 <div class="item"
04     *ngFor="let item of items">
05     <rated-item
```

```
06        [item]="item"
07        [ratingsService]="ratingsService">
08      </rated-item>
09 <div>
```

Listing 12.26 shows a CSS file that styles the `item` class on `app.component.html`.

Listing 12.26   `app.component.css`: **A CSS File That Styles the Application**

```
01 img {
01 .item{
02      border: .5px solid black;
03      display: inline-block;
04      width:175px;
05      text-align: center;
06 }
```

Listing 12.27 shows an Angular component that displays a rated item. Lines 13 through 15 define the `constructor` method, which initializes the `starArray` value.

Lines 18 through 20 define the `setRating` method, which takes the parameter `rating`. The method invokes the `updateRating` method on the `ratings` service and takes the parameters `item` and `rating`, which the ratings service uses to update the rating of the item.

Lines 21 through 27 define the `getStarClass` method, which takes the parameter `rating`. This method is used to assign the class of each star to accurately represent the rating of the item.

Listing 12.27   `rated-item.component.ts`: **An Angular Component That Displays an Image as Well as a Rating for the Image**

```
01 import { Component, OnInit, Input } from '@angular/core';
02 import { RatingsService } from '../ratings.service';
03
04 @Component({
05   selector: 'rated-item',
06   templateUrl: './rated-item.component.html',
07   styleUrls: ['./rated-item.component.css']
08 })
09 export class RatedItemComponent implements OnInit {
10   @Input ("item") item: any;
11   @Input ("ratingsService") ratingsService: RatingsService;
12   starArray: number[];
13   constructor() {
14     this.starArray = [1,2,3,4,5];
15   }
16   ngOnInit() {
17   }
```

```
18   setRating(rating){
19     this.ratingsService.updateRating(this.item, rating);
20   }
21   getStarClass(rating){
22     if(rating <= this.item.rating){
23       return "star";
24     } else {
25       return "empty";
26     }
27   }
28 }
```

Listing 12.28 shows an Angular template that displays a title, an image, and a rating. Lines 8 through 12 create the stars, which are used to visualize the rating. When a user clicks on a new rating, the overall rating is adjusted, using the setRating method. The getStarClass method determines whether the stars are filled in or blank.

Listing 12.28   `rated-item.component.html`: **An Angular Template That Displays a Title and an Image as Well as a Rating for the Image**

```
01 <p class="title">
02   {{item.title}}
03 </p>
04 <img src="{{item.url}}" />
05 <p>
06   Rating: {{item.rating}}
07 </p>
08 <span *ngFor="let rating of starArray"
09       (click)="setRating(rating)"
10       [ngClass]="getStarClass(rating)">
11    
12 </span>
```

Listing 12.29 shows a CSS file that styles the application by setting the dimensions of the rated item and adding stars to give that item a visualized rating.

Listing 12.29   `rated-item.component.css`: **A CSS File That Styles the Application**

```
01 * {
02     margin: 5px;
03 }
04 img {
05     height: 100px;
06 }
07 .title{
08   font: bold 20px/24px Verdana;
```

```
09 }
10 span {
11     float: left;
12     width: 20px;
13     background-repeat: no-repeat;
14     cursor: pointer;
15 }
16 .star{
17     background-image: url("../../assets/images/star.png");
18 }
19 .empty {
20     background-image: url("../../assets/images/empty.png");
21 }
```

Figure 12.4 shows the star rating component in the browser. Clicking on a star changes the rating in the mock back-end service, which updates the UI component.

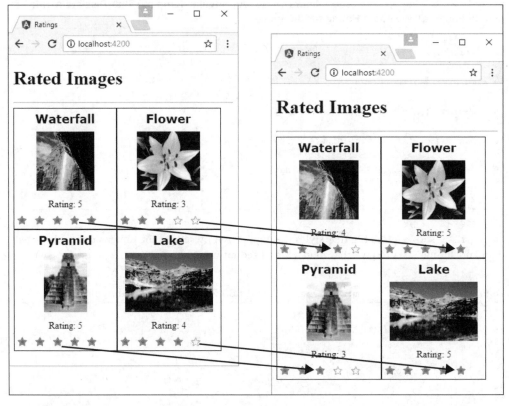

Figure 12.4   Using Angular components and services to implement star ratings on images with a mock back end

Summary

In this chapter, you got a chance to see how to extend what you have learned in the rest of the book to build some cool Angular components. You have seen how to implement animations, create a star rating component, and implement drag-and-drop capability. These are just some of the many ways to use Angular in real-world web applications. If you are interested in learning more about angular https://angular.io is a great resource.

Index

D

M